SAPPHO

WILLIS BARNSTONE is Associate Professor of Spanish and Comparative Literature at Indiana University. Born in Lewiston, Maine, he received his M.A. from Columbia and his Ph.D. from Yale. He is editor and translator of a volume of Greek lyric poetry, editor of an anthology of contemporary European poetry, and has translated a novel from modern Greek. Mr. Barnstone is the author of three books of poetry and in 1961 was a Guggenheim fellow in Spain, where he wrote a critical study of the Spanish poet Antonio Machado. A recent volume is his version in verse of the medieval Latin bestiary, *Physiologus Theobaldi*.

SAPPHO

Lyrics in the Original Greek
with Translations by
Willis Barnstone

FOREWORD BY ANDREW R. BURN

ANCHOR BOOKS
DOUBLEDAY & COMPANY, INC.
GARDEN CITY, NEW YORK

Anchor Books Edition: 1965

Library of Congress Catalog Card Number 64-16247

Copyright © 1965 by Willis Barnstone

Some of the translations appearing in the section
"Text and Translations" are reprinted from *Greek Lyric Poetry*,
copyright © 1962 by Bantam Books, Inc.

PUBLISHER'S NOTE TO THIS EDITION

This edition is intended to introduce the work of Sappho to the modern reader. It does not attempt the definitive text, which can be found in Lobel and Page's excellent edition, *Poetarum Lesbiorum Fragmenta*. In the hope that the reader may appreciate how much — or how little — of the available text requires tentative reconstruction to complete the poem, the translations are presented with the Greek from which they were derived on facing pages. The intention is to make Sappho accessible to the reader unfamiliar with Greek; yet the Greek text serves to remind one not only of the difficulties inherent in any translation but also of the problems implicit in establishing a reliable text. Some of the translations have, therefore, been derived from Edmonds' reconstructions on the grounds that only these yield to intelligible translation, though it is recognized that they are tentative. In each case that conjectural reconstructions have been used, however, these parts are enclosed in brackets.

FOREWORD

Simultaneous invention or discovery is a well-known phenomenon in history; the cases of Newton and Leibnitz, Darwin and A. R. Wallace are only the most striking of many. Indeed, since what H. G. Wells called the "invention of invention" in the time of Edison, occurrences have been frequent enough to keep a whole corps of patent lawyers in considerable affluence. In what one may call the Great Dialogue of man with his world, it will quite naturally happen from time to time that more than one fertile mind will simultaneously come out with the same observation, or arrive at the same answer or very similar answers to a problem.

It is therefore not — strictly speaking — surprising, though noteworthy, that in the immediate past two or more American scholars, working on the translation of Sappho, have offered rather similar, thoroughly contemporary solutions of the formidable problems presented. The translation included by Mr. Willis Barnstone in his edition of the complete extant work of Sappho, which it is a pleasure and privilege here to introduce, is less starkly antiromantic than the little translation of one hundred pieces by Miss Mary Barnard, published in 1958 in California; but both scholars are at one in the firm rejection of sentimentality and "prettiness." That is in the modern manner; and few (though perhaps a few) will deny that it is right.

The recovery of a few more poems in something like completeness, or at least of enough of them to give us their drift, among the desert-edge trash heaps and crocodile-mummy-stuffing of Alexandrian Egypt, has shown how thoroughly *occasional* much of Sappho's work was: poems,

probably turned out with great speed, not only for the
worship of gods and for great occasions such as weddings,
but on any occasion whatever. Several of her extant poems
and those of her friend or acquaintance Alkaios are letters;
real letters, not literary exercises. It is interesting to notice
that the practice of writing letters in verse is still not dead
among Greek peasants of Cyprus, whose language also
preserves archaic features. (One such, on the German para-
chutists' capture of Crete in 1941, became a war ballad in
Crete in its own right.) In such poetry we should not look
for elaborate "poetic diction" or for much that is far re-
moved from the language of daily life; though we cannot be
sure that there were *no* words in Sappho's vocabulary that
were used only in poetry, since Lesbian song probably had
a long preliterate tradition behind it.

A Swinburnian elaboration in translation clearly gets it
wrong; but how is one to get it right? Probably there is no
better method than, as here, in language only a little more
formal than common speech and not at all more formal
than careful prose. But it remains true that great poetry is
strictly not translatable at all. One always must lose the
sound, originally so intimately married to the sense; and to
replace what is lost by giving a poet, as was said of Gilbert
Murray's *Euripides*, "beauties which he never possessed in
the original," is cheating — though if it produces a version
readable in itself, much may be forgiven. To the Greekless
reader who would like to approach Sappho, it can only be
said that even to learn the Greek alphabet and to give the
vowels their Italian values will give something; and that to
learn (from a teacher; there are no manuals that I know
of) a little of the grammar of Lesbian Aeolic, it is not
necessary to go the long way around by learning first the
very different Greek of Athenian prose. But even then we
do not know and cannot now know the precise secret of
the accent, which in ancient Greek denoted pitch (*tonos*
— the word which we translate "accent" and use, in an
altered sense, as "tone"); the secret of the rise and fall of
the voice, such as can still be heard in Celtic languages; it
has been lost in modern Greek, no less than in English.

What a translation *can* give is all that we know of Sappho as a person. And this is something that we naturally want to know, after noting the enthusiasm, the *reverence*, nothing less, with which serious ancient Greeks, who had all she wrote at their disposal, speak of her. Plato, who could have been a great poet if his times had not made him a philosopher, was the first to call her — in a little poem — the Tenth Muse; and his Socrates cites her to Phaidros, as they walk by the Ilissos, as being among the great ones of old who were experts on love. Strabo, a grave, indeed a dull writer of the time of Augustus, a Stoic and a geographer, flashes with unwonted fire when he comes to Mytilene. Here, contemporary with Pittakos and Alkaios, lived Sappho, "a wonderful thing" (as we might say, "a phenomenon"); in all the centuries since, no poetess has approached her. Herodotos, born within a century of her death, gives one of the few valuable bits of tradition about her — and that, too, is based on her own writing; a poem, another letter-poem, in which she took to task her brother Charaxos, a young aristocrat out seeing the world, and trading in wine in order to do it. She chided him for wasting his money in liberating a slave courtesan of Naukratis, the Greek port in Egypt, who was thus enabled to remain in business on her account. It is all very sisterly. Herodotos gives incidentally Sappho's father's name as Skamandrōnymos, after Scamander, the river of Troy, where Mytilene had a colony; and there is no need to look further for this detail or to worry about alternative names given in the Byzantine encyclopedia called The Suda (or "Suidas," probably a ghost-name) — a muddled and unreliable compilation, produced nearer to our time than to Sappho's.

Most of the other and later ancient tradition about Sappho is deplorable stuff; Mr. Barnstone deals with it faithfully in his introduction. It derives largely from late-classical "Middle Comedy" of Athens, when, since contemporary political satire was no longer admissible, comic literary history was a popular source of plots, and obscenity was still a traditional feature. How far the comedians troubled about historical accuracy is shown by one play in which

Sappho has as suitors two other ancient poets, one of whom flourished sixty years before her and one sixty years later. But scholars seldom — in the second childhood of the ancient world — used these plays as a source.

What manner of person, then, is Sappho in her own poetry as we have it?

She is a married woman, with a daughter of her own, and a circle of younger girl friends. She is a poetess, respected, even revered, and sure of her fame. She writes hymns to the gods, especially Aphrodite, whom in her best-known poem she imagines smiling and asking her "Who is it *now*, Sappho?" (She takes herself a good deal less solemnly than most of her commentators have taken her.) And she writes passionately, tenderly, or, on occasion, with equally passionate jealousy, to or about her girls: poems for weddings, including presumably their weddings, with some heavy humor which we may suppose was traditional, and verse letters to girls who have gone away, one of them to live at Sardis in Lydia. Several of the girls are also reported to have come *from* overseas to Sappho's circle. Why did they come?

The only possible answer is that their parents sent them, to be with Sappho (or, it seems, with other ladies of Mytilene, including Andromeda, whom Sappho hated as a rival), as part of their education, before their early marriages. Mytilene was a center of culture, and women had a share in it. Sappho is not the only recorded poetess of Lesbos; and for the island's artistic standards, we have the firsthand evidence of its early coins, work of the most exquisite delicacy, far outclassing those, for instance, of Phokaia, the Ionian neighbor with which Mytilene had a currency convention. We are justified, then, in supposing that Sappho and other ladies of Mytilene *taught* girl-pupils from their own city and from others; taught them music, the art of poetry, and all other accomplishments suitable for a young lady of good family in that emancipated, east-Greek society, in which women had more social freedom than in old-world, conservative Athens. If so, then as head of her group Sappho must also have led them in worship

of the gods; and to this extent, even if he went beyond
the evidence in detail, Wilamowitz-Moellendorf was right
in speaking of her as head of a *thiasos* or religious grouping. Such a "family" in Greece without a common religious
life would be unthinkable.

And she loved her pupils; she loved at least some of
them, those whose names we have, passionately and erot-
ically. This is where modern discussion has found it difficult to "see straight." In the nineteenth century, either
Sappho had to be condemned as a "Lesbian," a mistress
(and presumably a teacher) of unnatural vice — and at
least one once influential history of Greek literature did
call her just that — or, in order to save her honor in the
eyes of respectable scholars, much in her fragmentary
known writings had to be explained away. It was largely
the chivalrous desire to save a lady's honor which led to
some exaggeration in Wilamowitz' theorising, when he
made her into a priestess. Our own day and age, whatever
its faults — and there can be no doubt that the freedom of
speech, and sex relations, in the modern West is something
for which many young people have paid and are paying
dearly — should be able to look clearly at Sappho, as at
the more fully recorded figure of Socrates.

It is no longer news to say that human beings are *normally*
more or less bisexual; a few very masculine or very feminine, and a very few other rare cases so precariously bal-
anced that the flesh may suffer a Teiresian change in the
course of a life. In most societies average normal men and
normal women have tended to despise the "feminine" or
effeminate man and to resent the masculine woman, though
some cultures have made a place for them; in most, the
real psychological differences between average men and
average women are accentuated by their conformity to
different traditional norms of behavior. Love of older
people for those younger of either sex, which is essential
for a good teacher, *normally* has a sexual element, though
that may be fiercely denied, and also certainly is not the
whole story; for instance, there is also a protective (pa-
rental) feeling, akin to that which any normal man will

have for a small bird or a kitten. A great teacher, now dead, once said to the writer that he thought only a physical pleasure in the company of young people could prevent the continual contact with immature minds from becoming intolerable; and another once shook me considerably by using the expression "the necessity of having favorites." It transpired that he meant exactly what I meant by "the necessity of *not* having favorites"; he explained that, if it is a pleasure to give of one's best in teaching David, who has fair hair and blue eyes, the teacher, for the sake of his self-respect, must give no less to little Tommy, who has pimples and thick spectacles. In Greece it was widely held that the right relation of a man (normally a married man) to a youth to whom he was attracted was that of a teacher of all virtue; the knight-and-squire relation of the poet Theognis of Negara (rather later than Sappho) to the young Kyrnos was considered a pattern; and Socrates differed from other people in this relation chiefly in being (as people felt, even in his circle) so startlingly frank about it.

It is not necessary or right to be starry-eyed about the Greeks in this connection. Generally speaking, they did not manage their sexual lives very well; though perhaps not so badly as the West, with the help of all-pervading corruption by press, cinema, and the advertising industry, is doing at present. Strict heterosexual conventions are not a sufficient protection against the spoiling and vulgarizing of a beautiful thing. Nor was every Greek a Socrates, or even a Sappho or a Theognis; and many attractive young people were very thoroughly spoilt, becoming adept in the game of "playing up" one admirer against another for the extraction of presents and attentions. "Though now she rejects your gifts, soon she will be giving them," says Aphrodite to Sappho. Kyrnos, too, was not always loyal. There was always the uninhibited jealousy, which pagan ethics and religion did not condemn and gave no reason for repressing. Sappho's attacks on Andromeda are not pretty. She felt jealous and did not disguise it, even when her girls were betrothed and married; but that was part of the course of nature, and she put up with it. To be abandoned, as sometimes happened, for another woman — we guess, but are not explicitly told, for another teacher — was "The End."

Nevertheless, however checkered the "bitter-sweetness" of which she speaks, her relations with her girls were the center of the life that produced so much golden poetry. The evidence is ample that girls came from overseas, from other islands and from cities of Ionia to be with her — she had an "international reputation." And though Greek parents most certainly were not indifferent to the honor, the morals and reputation of their children, there is no hint that any of them ever thought Sappho a corrupting influence. Her public speech is franker than any that a modern woman could permit herself; and, that, apart from Sappho's genius, is the chief difference.

A. R. Burn
SENIOR LECTURER IN
ANCIENT HISTORY

University of Glasgow
1963

ACKNOWLEDGMENTS

I wish to express my appreciation to the following owners of copyright material who have granted me permission to include selections from their editions of Sappho's poetry in this volume:

From *Lyra Graeca*, Volumes I and III, newly edited and translated by J. M. Edmonds. Reprinted by permission of Harvard University Press and the Loeb Classical Library.

From *Poetarum Lesbiorum Fragmenta*, Edgar Lobel and Denys Page, editors; *Sappho and Alcaeus: An Introduction to the Study of Ancient Lesbian Poetry*, by Denys Page; *Greek Lyric Poetry from Alcman to Simonides*, by Sir Cecil Maurice Bowra. Reprinted by permission of The Clarendon Press, Oxford.

From *Sappho*, by Max Treu. Reprinted by permission of the author and of Ernst Heimeran Verlag, Munich.

From *Anthologia Lyrica Graeca* (1934), Edward Diehl, editor. Reprinted by permission of Teubner Press, Leipzig.

Willis Barnstone

CONTENTS

INTRODUCTION

In Sappho we hear for the first time in the Western
world the direct words of an individual woman. We hear
the immediate sound of lyric poetry, the voice in solitude.
It cannot be said that her song has ever been surpassed.

It need not surprise us that the first woman poet should
have written with such candid passion, power, and simplicity, and with such singular individuality; for as a
woman she wrote from her privileged position as a minor
outsider in a busy male society. Outside the main business
of the world — of war, politics, remunerative work — Sappho
could speak with feeling of her own human world: of her
apprehension of nature, the experience of love, and of herself. She wrote giving the impression of complete involve-
ment, though even in her most intensely self-revealing
poems her words have the jarring strength of detachment
and accuracy. She wrote as one might speak, if one could
speak in perfect, simple speech. It may be noted that, while
the first man in Western literary history, Homer, is but
shadowed in his poetry (and considered with confidence by
some only as a bardic tradition), the first woman, Sappho,
despite a scanty biographical tradition, emerges through
her poetry as a completely realized personality. Homer was
of the epic-heroic tradition, but it took a lyric age to produce the first woman poet.[1]

Sappho was born in Lesbos, an island in the Aegean, a

[1] Archilochos had preceded Sappho by some fifty years as the
first man to whom we can attribute a significant body of extant
lyric poetry.

few miles off the coast of Asia Minor. Lesbos was — as it is today — a beautiful island, spotted with five coastal cities that commanded their harbors from a rocky acropolis. Greece is a country of light and rock and sea — its beauty and poverty — and shows off almost joyfully its few precious bits of fertile land. Lesbos was unusual in having a large part of its terrain tillable, along with its salt flats, dry hills, then wooded, and a 3,000-ft. mountain called Olympos after the traditional abode of the gods in Thessaly.[2] It was known in ancient times for its grain and fruit trees and above all the large valleys of olive groves. In 2500 years the island has probably changed very little in its village architecture and landscape. As one should know Baeza and Soria to understand Machado, or Vermont to know Frost, so there is no better way to know the images of Sappho's poetry than to see today the light and sea and land of Mytilene.

The biographical tradition of Sappho begins after her death and is a mixture of possible fact, contradiction, gossip, and myth. (Virtually all the sources are contained in the *Testimonia*.) From this at least some statements of probable truth may be made. Sappho's birthplace in Lesbos was Eresos or Mytilene; in any case, it is in Mytilene that she spent most of her life. She was born in or before 612 B.C. Her name in Attic Greek was Sappho *(Σαπφώ)*, by which she is known, but in her native Aiolic she called herself Psappho *(Ψάπφω)*.[3] She wrote as she spoke, and the speech of Lesbos was Aiolic Greek.[4]

Her father's name was given by Herodotus as Skamandronymos; but it appears also as Skamandros or Skamon or

[2] Mt. Olympos, 3,077 feet, highest mountain of Lesbos; not to be confused with the mainland home of the gods.

[3] The name also appears less correctly as Sáppho (Σάπφω), Saphphó (Σαφφώ), and Saphó (Σαφώ).

[4] This dialect differed from Attic, for example, in preserving the original long *a* and the digamma F, shifting the accent near the beginning of a word and resisting the change of *p* into *t*.

Eunominos or Eurygyos or Euarchos or Ekrytos or Semos. Her mother's name was Kleïs. Some suggest — and some deny — that she married a rich merchant from Andros named Kerkolas or Kerkylas, who may have been the father of her daughter Kleïs. She had two brothers, perhaps three: Charaxos, Larichos, and possibly, the more shadowy Eurygyos. Several poems speak disapprovingly of Charaxos, a young man who paid for voyages abroad by trading wine off his estates, and who had spent large sums of family money to buy the freedom in Egypt of a courtesan named Doricha. Larichos was a public cup-bearer in Mytilene. We know nothing of Eurygyos, if he indeed existed.

As for her personal appearance, there are no statues, coins, or vase paintings until long after her death. But she was frequently referred to as the "beautiful Sappho," and with the same authority she was described as short, dark, and ugly, "like a nightingale with misshapen wings." In the existing statues and coins she is usually depicted with the idealized features and beauty of Aphrodite.

The evidence of her activities is not more conclusive. Sappho lived during the reigns of three tyrants in Lesbos: Melanchros, Myrsilos, and Pittakos the Sage. When she was young, it appears that she and her family went, for political reasons first, under Myrsilos, to the Lesbian hill city of Pyrrha, and later to Syracuse in Sicily, probably in the time of Pittakos. To have left for political reasons implies that her family was important in city affairs.

The girls mentioned as her companions were Anaktoria, Atthis, Gyrrino (or Gyrinna), Gongyla, Mnasidika and Mika and Dika (diminutives of Mnasidika), Erinna, Telesippa, Megara, and Anagora; she was angry with Gorgo and Andromeda who had left her to become rivals. But the widely held theory of Wilamowitz that her relationship to these girls was that of high priestess in a cult-association (*thiasos*), or a girls' academy, has no basis in the ancient biographical tradition and no support in the existing remains of her poems. The ancient commentators have also told us that there were really two Sapphos, one a poet and one a prostitute who also wrote poems, or that Sappho herself was a prostitute, and they recount the legend that she threw herself from the Leukadian cliffs out of love for the ferryman Phaon. It should be remembered when considering these more extravagant tales that there were at least six plays dealing with Sappho in later Attic comedy[5] and that by then she had become a stock figure on the Athenian stage. It was on the stage, her modern apologists contend, that the black legend of Sappho originated.

Sappho is credited with certain technical innovations. She is said to have been the first to use the *pectis* (a kind of harp), and to have invented the Mixolydian mode and the Sapphic stanza, which was imitated by Horace and Catullus. A Sapphic stanza, as in the ode to Aphrodite (30), reads:[6]

$$- \cup - \text{x} - \cup \cup - \cup - -$$
$$- \cup - \text{x} - \cup \cup - \cup - -$$
$$- \cup - \text{x} - \cup \cup - \cup - -$$
$$- \cup \cup - -$$

We have good reason to believe that Sappho was a prolific writer. We do not know how she recorded her work — whether on papyrus, on wooden tablets overlaid with wax, or orally through song — but centuries later, when the Alexandrian grammarians arranged her work according to meter into nine books, the first book contained 1320 lines (330 four-line stanzas in Sapphics); judging from this, we may suppose that the nine books contained a very extensive

---

[5] Plays by Ameipsias, Amphis, Antiphanes, Diphilos, Ephippos, and Timokles.

[6] Sappho was not the first Lesbian to contribute innovations to Greek poetry. Before her were the semi-legendary poets Arion and Lesches and then Terpandros, who invented, and wrote poetry for, the seven-string lyre, of whom we have four small and doubtful fragments, the earliest examples of lyric poetry in Greece. Her contemporary Alkaios wrote Alcaics, which were also imitated by Horace and other Latin poets. For further discussion of meter, see metrical tables and index, p. 189.

opus. Her work was well known and well preserved in antiquity. We have Athenaios's claim in the third century A.D. that he knew all of Sappho's lyrics by heart. But the best indication, perhaps, of the general availability of her works in the classical age is in the number of quotations from her poems by grammarians, even late into Roman times, which suggests that both commentator and reader had ready access to the corpus of the work being quoted.

Of the more than five hundred poems by Sappho, we have today about seven hundred intelligible lines, and these come from no single collected copy but are pieced together from many sources: from the scholia of ancient grammarians to the mummy wrappings in Egyptian tombs. Plato's entire work has survived virtually intact, having been both popular with and approved by pagan and Christian alike. Sappho's work did not lack popularity; but as one who, in Ovid's words, "taught how to love girls" (*Lesbia quid docuit Sappho nisi amare puellas?*), her popularity did not always win approval.

To the Church mind Sappho represented the culmination of moral laxity, and her work was treated with zealous disapproval. About 380 A.D. St. Gregory of Nazianzos, Bishop of Constantinople, ordered the burning of Sappho's writings wherever found. She had already been violently attacked as early as 180 A.D. by the Assyrian ascetic Tatian: "Sappho was a whorish woman, love-crazy, who sang about her own licentiousness."

Σαπφὼ γύναιον πορνικὸν ἐρωτομανὲς καὶ
τὴν ἑαυτῆς ἀσέλγειαν ἄδει.
(*Orat. ad Graec.* 53)

Then in 391 a mob of Christian zealots partially destroyed the classical library in Alexandria of Ptolemy Soter. The often repeated story of the final destruction of this famous library by the Arab general Amr and Caliph Omar is now rejected by historians. Again we hear that in 1073 Sappho's

writings were publicly burned in Rome and Constantinople
by order of Pope Gregory VII. Until late in the eleventh
century, however, quotations from Sappho still appeared
in the works of grammarians, suggesting that copies of her
poems were still preserved. We shall never know how many
poems by Sappho were destroyed in April 1204 during the
terrible pillage of Constantinople by the Venetian knights
of the Fourth Crusade, or by the Ottoman Turks at the fall
of Byzantium in 1453.

But apart from official hostility, Sappho's works suffered
equally from the general decline of learning in the early
Middle Ages and the consequent ravages of time upon
neglected manuscripts. It is probable that some of her
work was lost circa the ninth century when classical texts,
preserved in uncial script, were selected and recopied in
modern letters. No single collection of her poems, in whole
or in part, survived the medieval period. Nevertheless, in
the Renaissance, Sappho came back into light. Italian scholars found Longinus's *Essay on the Sublime* and Dionysios
of Halikarnassos's *Treatise on Style*, which contain two of
her most important poems: "Seizure" (9) and the complete
ode "A Prayer to Aphrodite" (28). Every stanza, line, and
even isolated word by Sappho that appeared in the works of
other Greek and Latin writers was assembled. But there
was little hope of finding original papyrus manuscripts in
Greece, for papyrus, unlike the more durable parchment,
could not easily survive in even the dry climate of Greece.[7]

Only in waterless parts of Egypt, in the rubbish heaps of
antiquity, could the ancient documents still be preserved,
buried in tombs or with ancient cities under the sand. In
the Fayum, an oasis semi-detached from the Nile valley
near Crocodilopolis, important eighth-century manuscripts

[7] In 1961, for the first time, original papyrus was found in
continental Greece, at Dervani (Lagada). See Herbert Hunger
"Papyrusfund in Griechenland," *Chronique D'Egypte*, tome
XXXVII, No. 74, Brussels, July, 1962.

with poems by Sappho were discovered in 1879. The Egyptian expeditions by the English scholars Grenfell and Hunt, beginning in 1897, yielded a wealth of material. In addition to important poems by Sappho, parts of four plays of Menandros were found in a refuse heap near Aphroditopolis; at Oxyrhynchos, Alkman's maiden-song choral ode, the first in Greek literature, and twenty odes by Bakchylides were discovered. Sappho ceased to be simply a name and became a major poet, to rival Pindar.

But above all, the range of Sappho's work was dramatically expanded. The precious papyri were used as papier-mâché in mummy wrapping; unfortunately, many were torn in vertical strips, and as a result the Sappho fragments are mutilated at the beginning or end of lines, if not in the middle. The mummy-makers of Egypt transformed much of Sappho into columns of words, syllables, or single letters, and so made her poems look, at least typographically, like Apollinaire and e. e. cummings.

```
΄.]δη[
΄.]κωσα[
  ]ν.οοι[
 ].δηκ.[
 ]εσιππ[
 ].αλ.[
 ].εσσα[
].[.].[⁸
```

But the price of this unwitting modernization was the loss of intelligibility of many fragments. The cost was also

⁸ Ezra Pound goes back full circle when he "antiques" the form of a poem in order to make it resemble a vertical strip of a Sappho papyrus. The brief poem "Papyrus," addressed to Gongyla, reads:

> Spring . . .
> Too long . . .
> Gongula . . .

high to the English and German scholars who undertook the labor of unraveling the documents (both literally and figuratively): the German scholar Friedrich Blass, who first deciphered important poems by Sappho in the Fayum manuscript, lost the use of his eyes, and Grenfell, for a while, lost his mind. It has been the modern commentators, however, who, in their enthusiasm for Sappho, have quite lost their perspective of the poet and have hopelessly muddled the poet's life with the poems.

While a thousand years of bigotry destroyed the greater part of Sappho's poetry, the zeal of her later defenders, from Anna Le Fevee Dacier in 1682 to Wilamowitz, Snell, and Bowra[9], to rehabilitate her moral character has not helped the poet's cause, nor has it contributed to our understanding of her work. It is no less than astonishing how otherwise temperate scholars become outraged, blindly indignant, and imaginatively unobjective at the slightest suggestion by others of moral frivolity on Sappho's part. Not Sappho's poems, but Middle and New Comedy and Horace and Ovid are accused of incepting the black legend.

Several arguments are offered and reiterated to justify her love poems to other women: Sappho was a priestess and head of a *thiasos* and these poems did not mean literally what they say; her love poems to women were epithalamia written for ceremonial purposes; the poems castigating her brother Charaxos for his affair with Doricha prove her own high virtue; Alkaios once addressed her as ἄγνα (holy or chaste); she came from a noble and highly respectable Lesbian family. The arguments read like a brief — in an unnecessary trial.

Almost alone, Denys Page has chosen to oppose all this. Page, who with Lobel has produced the most authoritative edition of Sappho's works, chose to look at the texts and found that the poems gave no support whatsoever to the

[9] Bowra modifies his defense in the 1962 edition of *Greek Lyric Poetry*.

arguments; moreover, Page contends: Sappho was not a high priestess, only a small portion of her poems might be considered epithalamia, and Sappho herself, far from being a woman of unfailingly noble sentiments, was a common mortal concerned with common matters of love and jealousy. In deflating the contentions of her supporters, Page also deflates Sappho herself — not without a note of moral reproach.

I have spent some time reviewing the history of Sappho's usually violent encounter with the world, not because one must necessarily know something or anything about an author to appreciate his work, but because in Sappho's case the world has known — or assumed — too much, and this knowledge interferes with any fair appraisal of her poems. The crucial question has been whether or not Sappho was indeed a Lesbian in the sexual, as well as in the geographical, sense of the word.

First, it should be stated that whatever Sappho was in her life has very little to do with the content of her poetry; whether she was indeed homosexual or merely ascetic like her contemporaries Jeremiah and Gautama Siddhartha will not change the meaning of her poems. It is not that an author's intention must be discounted, nor need we puristically fear the modern heresy of "intentional fallacy" or other critical sins; but if the author's intention is meaningful, it must be seen through the poem, through the lyrical speaker in the poem, and not merely from outside sources. In Sappho's case the problem is more rudimentary; for even if we could accept outside authority, there is, in fact, no reliable authority outside the poems themselves to explain the author's intended meaning in her many poems dealing with love.

To find Sappho then — the Sappho of the poems — we must look at the poems themselves. A few of them may have been addressed to men. The majority are love poems to women. They are passionate poems, self-critical, self-revealing, detached, and intense. If we are to believe what they say, we will conclude that the speaker in the poems experienced a physical passion for her beloved, with all the sexual implications that similar poems between men and women normally imply.[10] To give to the poems meanings which the texts do not support, for whatever moral motive, is to dilute her language and to weaken and falsify her work. Even though the remains of her poems are scant, it is the poems which should be allowed to speak for Sappho and not the theories of later interpretors.

Sappho's best-known love poem, "Seizure" (9), imitated by Catullus, is an example of her control, precision, objectivity, economy, and accumulative power: in short, all her abstract virtues as a poet. The poem is simple, direct, self-revealing, yet detached and calmly accurate at the moment of highest fever. She begins with a poised statement of her jealousy of the man sitting near the girl she loves, who, because of his envied position, appears godlike to her; she recounts the physical symptoms of her passion for the girl; and with full intensity but without exaggeration she uses the metaphor of pale grass to show her suffering, verging on death, because of a love not returned:

> To me that man equals a god
> as he sits before you and listens
> closely to your sweet voice
>
> and lovely laughter — which troubles
> the heart in my ribs. For now
> as I look at you my voice fails,
>
> my tongue is broken and thin fire
> runs like a thief through my body.
> My eyes are dead to light, my ears

[10] This will not seem so unusual when we recall that the majority of Greek love poems by male poets, from Ibykos to Pindar, are addressed to other men.

pound, and sweat pours down over me.
I shudder, I am paler than grass
and am intimate with dying — but

I must suffer everything, being poor.[11]

The poem states a love relationship, but more, it states
the poet's desperation when, consumed by love, she can in
no way — except through words — escape from the solitude
in which she is suddenly enclosed, as her senses fail her
and she can no longer see, speak, or hear. Her moment near
death is an analogue of the *via negativa*. Like San Juan
de la Cruz in *"El cántico espiritual,"* in her suffering she
reaches a momentary detachment from bodily senses in
which she can speak objectively of her passion. As an accurate outside observer, as it were, she avoids all sentimentality. The universal condition she describes is a passion and
ecstasy[12] found in other poems, from the Canticles to San
Juan, Marvell, and Guillén. But hers is love's inferno and
illumination without the union or the peace that follows.

Unable to reach the object of her love, there is no ful-
fillment and no release except in the poem. Yet in her
poetry she does indeed reach the world, if not her beloved.
Her words, used masterfully, make the reader one with the
poet so that he may share her vision of herself. There is
no veil between poet and reader. Here, as elsewhere in her
art, Sappho makes the lyric poem a refined and precise
instrument for revealing her personal and intense experience of life.

[11] See note on last line in *Notes* on the poems.

[12] For an interesting and full examination of the condition of
transport, see Margharita Laski, *Ecstasy, A Study of Some Secu-
lar and Religious Experiences,* Indiana University Press, Bloom-
ington, 1962.

I wish to thank Professors William McCulloh of Kenyon College, James Halporn of Indiana University, Charles Adams of the University of Massachusetts, and Maurianne Adams of Smith College for their help in preparing the manuscript. William McCulloh both suggested and prepared the metrical index. Helle Phaedra Barnstone was of constant and invaluable help in the long preparation of the many parts of this book.

ARRANGEMENT OF THE POEMS AND TEXTS

It is said that the metrical arrangement of Sappho's poems into nine books was the work of Alexandrian scholars, perhaps the grammarians Aristophanes and Aristarchos, though all this, including the number nine, is disputed. There is surely nothing to indicate that Sappho herself followed a plan similar to that of the late Alexandrians, or indeed that she arranged her poems in any order. Nevertheless, in most modern editions, it has been customary to divide her fragments into nine sections, the last of which is the epithalamia. I have disregarded previous arrangements, and followed an arbitrary esthetic order, based on subject and an implied chronology of the speaker in the poems from youth to maturity. Thus, poems on nature or to Atthis or Aphrodite or brides generally stand together, and the speaker at the end of the poems seems older and perhaps more grave than the voice in the first poems. The collection ends with two brief love lyrics.

The texts used are mainly Lobel & Page, Diehl, Edmonds ings: Bowra in *Greek Lyric Poetry*, Robinson, and Page in his *Sappho and Alcaeus*. Page has been freer in reconstructing the Greek tests in his *Sappho and Alcaeus* than in the text he edited with Lobel. In the *Sources and Notes* only the primary, not the many secondary, sources for the Greek texts are listed. These, as well as variant readings, appear in full detail in Lobel & Page, Treu and Diehl. While the Lobel & Page *Poetarum Lesbiorum Fragmenta* is rightly conservative in regard to even obvious emendations, it remains the most nearly complete Greek text of Sappho's poems. To reproduce here what already appears in great detail in Lobel & Page would merely duplicate their work and is, in any case, beyond the scope of this volume. The reader interested in variant readings will turn directly to Lobel & Page. The reader interested in English translations is not likely to be concerned with the massive scholarship in Lobel & Page's exemplary volume; but if he has some knowledge of Greek, and wishes to see how these English translations were arrived at, or wishes to use them as an aid to his own translations, then the accompanying Greek in this edition should be useful.

I have usually followed Treu's *Sappho*,[1] whenever his more recent volume attributes a poem to Sappho which Diehl or Lobel & Page assign to Alkaios. And where I have followed Edmonds, it is usually for his emendations, or for a text which he has extracted from an indirect quotation.

Most of Edmonds' emendations are small and obvious. They do not occur in Lobel & Page, because the purpose of that edition was to set down the Greek text, and no more, in so far as it can be read. Had Page included more Sappho poems in his *Sappho and Alcaeus*, where he both interprets and translates the Greek poems, he might have emended them to the same degree to which he did emend those which do appear there; in *Sappho and Alcaeus* Page goes about as far as Bowra in his *Greek Lyric Poetry* to repair the Greek texts. Treu takes greater liberties than either Page or Bowra, and Edmonds more than any one of the three, in matters of restoration.

Edmonds takes badly mutilated fragments and, by metrical and stylistic reasoning and considerable conjecture, fills in some of the gaps. He also extracts Greek texts from indirect quotations. At times, he makes *exempli gratia* sup-

[1] The most complete casebook on Sappho for the reader acquainted with German is Max Treu's *Sappho*, Munich, 1958. It contains Greek text, variant readings, sources, notes, translations, indirect quotations of poems, ancient testimonia, bibliography and a study of Sappho. The translations are accurate and pleasantly old-fashioned. Treu makes a strong argument for Sappho's authorship of some fragments attributed by most scholars, including Diehl and Lobel & Page, to Alkaios. Treu's work is an invaluable source for Sappho studies.

plements. Whenever his supplemented and emended text
is used in this edition, care has been taken to distinguish
emendations from the basic text, or to identify a poem as
an indirect quotation.[2] Edmonds' use of the iota subscript
and Diehl and Lobel-Page's placement of it on the side are
followed. Lobel-Page's use of the dagger symbol, denoting
uncertain passages, has not been followed.

No one since Edmonds, with the possible exception of
Treu, has attempted the difficult, useful but thankless tasks
of rescuing texts from the oblivion of unintelligibility. In
this volume, where no new Greek text is offered but rather
an attempt to present a literary version of Sappho in English, I have gone to Edmonds for his restorations in those
few cases where the alternative was the complete loss of
the poem.[3]

While I have gratefully turned to Bowra's and Page's
emended texts in *Greek Lyric Poetry* and *Sappho and
Alcaeus*, and to Edmonds in *Lyra Graeca* for more extensive restorations when the alternative was omission, in
many cases, however — where the Greek text at first appeared to be irretrievably mutilated — I have disregarded
all conjectural supplements and tried to decipher a meaning from the unrestored text alone. It is the first time, to
my knowledge, that these particular unrestored fragments
have been translated into English verse. The results have

[2] Most translations into English from Greek lyric poetry in
the last forty years, including the recent excellent versions
by Barnard and Roche from Sappho, and those by Lattimore
and Fagles from Bakchylides, have depended on the Edmonds
restorations, as they appear in Loeb Library editions. Lattimore
writes: "For restorations to fill out the text of Bacchylides, I am
indebted to the editions of Blass, Jebb, Kenyon, Snell, and
particularly Edmonds. I also take this occasion to acknowledge
my gratitude to the great company of true scholars who have
collected, edited, pieced out, and interpreted all the texts which
have been used in these translations." *Greek Lyrics*, Chicago,
1960.

[3] Reference is not made to the majority of those texts by Edmonds used in this volume where a simple emendation or the
unscrambling of an indirect quotation, rather than extensive
restoration, determined the choice of his text.

been at least personally gratifying. In such cases one does not fill in words — as in restorations — but guesses at syntactical relationships of isolated words and phrases. In either method, of course, there is more than an element of conjecture. But these unrestored fragments, when so deciphered, have, to my mind, in their necessary bareness, a stark modernity which makes them particularly effective and suggestive of Sappho's power and concision. I wish that this latter method of translation were possible in every case where the original text at first seemed hauntingly unintelligible.

And finally, the reader should be reminded that the titles of the poems are supplied by the translator, and the particular source for the text of each poem is designated in bold type. Notes to the poems appear at the back of the book.

W.B.

BIBLIOGRAPHY

Bowra, Sir Cecil M. *Greek Lyric Poetry*. 2d ed. Oxford. 1961.

Diehl, Ernest. *Anthologia Lyrica Graeca*, Vol. I. Leipzig. 1935.

Edmonds, J. M. *Lyra Graeca*, Vol. I, III. (Loeb Classical Library), London. 1928.

Lobel, Edgar. *ΣΑΠΦΟΥΣ ΜΕΛΗ(Σμ)*. Oxford. 1925.

Lobel, Edgar and Denys Page. *Poetarum Lesbiorum Fragmenta*. Oxford. 1955.

Miller, Marion M. and David M. Robinson. *The Songs of Sappho*. Lexington. 1925.

Page, Denys. *Sappho and Alcaeus*. Oxford. 1955.

Treu, Max. *Sappho*. München. 1958.

SAPPHO

For Helle Phaedra

ἰόπλοκ' ἄγνα μελλιχόμειδε Σάπφοι

Violet-haired, pure, honey-smiling Sappho

ALKAIOS

TEXT AND TRANSLATIONS

1

ἄγε δῖα χέλυννά μοι
φωνάεσσά τε γίγνεο

D 103, **E 80**, LP 118

2

ἀερίων ἐπέων ἄρχομαι ἀλλ᾽ ὀνάτων

E 1α

3

– – – θος· ἀ γάρ με γέννα . . .
– – ας ἐπ᾽ ἀλικίας μεγ . . .
[κ]όσμον αἴ τις ἔχη[ι] φόβα . . .
πορφύρωι κατελιξαμε[ν] . . .
ἔμμεναι μάλα τοῦτο . . .
ἀλλα ξανθοτέρα[ι] ἔχη . . .
τα[ὶ]ς κόμα[ι]ς δάιδος προ . . .
[σ]τεφάνοισιν ἐπαρτια . . .
ἀνθέων ἐριθαλέων
[μ]ιτράναν δ᾽ ἀρτίως κλ . . .
ποικίλαν ἀπὺ Σαρδίω[ν] . . .
– – – – αονιασπολεις . . .

D. Suppl. pp. 39, 70, **LP 98α**

THE LYRIC POEM

Come, holy tortoise shell,
my lyre, and become a poem.

NOW I BEGIN

I begin with words of air
yet they are good to hear.

HEADDRESS

My mother always said
that in her youth she was
exceedingly in fashion

wearing a purple ribbon
looped in her hair. But
the girl whose hair is yellower

than torchlight need wear no
colorful ribbons from Sardis —
but a garland of fresh flowers.

4

ἀλλά τις οὐκ ἔμμι παλιγκότων
ὄργαν, ἀλλ' ἀβάκην τὰν φρέν' ἔχω . . .

D 108, E 74, LP 120

5

Οἰ μὲν ἰππήων στρότον οἰ δὲ πέσδων
οἰ δὲ νάων φαῖσ' ἐπὶ γᾶν μέλαιναν
ἔμμεναι κάλλιστον· ἔγω δὲ κῆν' ὄτ-
τω τις ἔραται.

πάγχυ δ' εὔμαρες σύνετον πόησαι
πάντι τοῦτ'· ἀ γὰρ πόλυ περσκέθοισα
[κάλ]λος ἀνθρώπων Ἐλένα τὸν ἄνδρα
[κρίννεν ἄρ]ιστον

[ὄς τὸ πὰν] σέβας Τροίας ὄλεσσε,
[κωὐδὲ πα]ῖδος οὐδὲ φίλων τοκήων
[μᾶλλον] ἐμνάσθη, ἀλλὰ παράγαγ' αὔταν
[πῆλε φίλει]σαν

[Ὤρος· εὖκ]αμπτον γὰρ [ἀεὶ τὸ θῆλ]υ
[αἴ κέ] τις κούφως τ[ὸ πάρον ν]οήσῃ·
[ἄμ]με νῦν, Ἀνακτορία, [σ]ὺ μέμναι-
[σ' οὐ] παρεοίσαις,

[τᾶ]ς κε βολλοίμαν ἔρατόν τε βᾶμα
κἀμάρυχμα λάμπρον ἴδην προσώπω
ἤ τὰ Λύδων ἄρματα κὰν ὄπλοισι
[πεσδομ]άχεντας.

D 27, E 38, LP 16

HER INNOCENCE

I do not have a rancorous spirit
but the simple heart of a child.

TO ANAKTORIA

Some say cavalry and others claim
infantry or a fleet of long oars
is the supreme sight on the black earth.
                    I say it is

the one you love. And easily proved.
Did not Helen, who was queen of mortal
beauty, choose as first among mankind
                    the very scourge

of Trojan honor? Haunted by Love
she forgot kinsmen, her own dear child,
and wandered off to a remote country.
                    Weak and fitful

woman bending before any man!
So Anaktoria, although you are
far, do not forget your loving friends.
                    And I for one

would rather listen to your soft step
and see your radiant face — than watch
all the dazzling chariots and armored
                    hoplites of Lydia.

6

Δέδυκε μὲν ἀ σέλαννα
καὶ Πληΐαδες, μέσαι δὲ
νύκτες, παρὰ δ᾽ ἔρχετ᾽ ὤρα,
ἔγω δὲ μόνα κατεύδω.

D 94, **E 111**

7

ὄπταις ἄμμε

D 19, E 27, **LP 38**

8

Ἔρος δ᾽ ἐτίναξέ μοι
φρένας, ὠς ἄνεμος κὰτ ὄρος δρύσιν ἐμπέτων.

D 50, E 54, **LP 47**

ALONE

The moon and Pleiades
are set. Night is half
gone and time speeds by.
I lie in bed, alone.

TO EROS

You burn me.

THE BLAST OF LOVE

Like a mountain whirlwind
punishing the oak trees
love shattered my heart.

9

Φαίνεταί μοι κῆνος ἴσος θέοισιν
ἔμμεν ὤνηρ ὄττις ἐνάντιός τοι
ἰζάνει καὶ πλάσιον ἆδυ φωνεί-
σας ὑπακούει

καὶ γελαίσας ἰμμέροεν, τό μ᾽ ἦ μὰν
κάρζαν ἐν στήθεσσιν ἐπεπτόασεν·
ὠς γὰρ ἔς τ᾽ ἴδω, βρόχε᾽, ὤς με φώνας
οὐδὲν ἔτ᾽ ἴκει,

ἀλλὰ κὰμ μὲν γλῶσσα Ϝέαγε, λέπτον
δ᾽ αὔτικα χρῷ πῦρ ὑπαδεδρόμακεν,
ὀππάτεσσι δ᾽ οὐδὲν ὄρημ᾽, ἐπιρρόμ-
βεισι δ᾽ ἄκουαι,

ἀ δέ μ᾽ ἴδρως κακχέεται, τρόμος δὲ
παῖσαν ἄγρη, χλωροτέρα δὲ ποίας
ἔμμι, τεθνάκην δ᾽ ὀλίγω ᾽πιδεύϝην
φαίνομαι·—ἀλλὰ

πάντ[α νῦν τ]ολμάτε᾽, ἐπεὶ ᾽πένησα . . .

D 2, **E 2**, LP 31, P 2

10

ψαύην δ᾽ οὐ δοκίμοιμ᾽ ὀράνω δύσι πάχεσι

D 47, **E 53**, LP 52

SEIZURE

To me that man equals a god
as he sits before you and listens
closely to your sweet voice

and lovely laughter — which troubles
the heart in my ribs. For now
as I look at you my voice fails,

my tongue is broken and thin fire
runs like a thief through my body.
My eyes are dead to light, my ears

pound, and sweat pours down over me.
I shudder, I am paler than grass,
and am intimate with dying — but

I must suffer everything, being poor.

WORLD

I could not hope
to touch the sky
with my two arms.

11

χρύσειοι δ᾽ ἐρέβινθοι ἐπ᾽ ἀιόνων ἐφύοντο

D 118, E 139, **LP 143**

12

μὴ κίνη χέραδος

D 113, E 78, **LP 145**

13

. . . τάδε νῦν ἐταίραις
ταῖς ἔμαισι τέρπνα κάλως ἀείσω

D 11, **E 12,** LP 160

14

Ἄστερες μὲν ἀμφὶ κάλαν σελάνναν
ἂψ ἀπυκρύπτοισι φάεννον εἶδος,
ὄπποτα πλήθοισα μάλιστα λάμπησ᾽
ἀργυρία γᾶν.

D 4, **E 3,** LP 34

BEACH COLOR

The furzy flower of the golden broom
grew along the shore.

LET SLEEPING DOGS LIE

Don't stir up the small
heaps of beach jetsam.

TO HER GIRL FRIENDS

On this day I will sing beautifully
and make you happy, dear comrades.

FULL MOON

The glow and beauty of the stars
are nothing near the splendid moon
when in her roundness she burns silver
about the world.

15

ἀρτίως μ᾽ ἀ χρυσοπέδιλλος αὔως
[ἦλθε καὶ] . . .

D 15, **E 19**, LP 123

16

. . . πτερύγων δ᾽ ὐπακακχέει
λιγύραν ἀοίδαν, ὄποτα φλόγι
[ὀ θέ]ος κατέτα [γάα]ν
ἐπι[πε]πτάμενος καταύγη . . .

D Alc. 94, **E 94**, LP Alc. 347b

17

γαῖσι . . . ψῦχρος μὲν ἔγεντ᾽ ὀ θῦμος
πὰρ δ᾽ ἴεισι τὰ πτέρα

D 13, E 16, **LP 42**

THEN

In gold sandals
dawn like a thief
fell upon me.

THE CRICKET

When sun dazzles the earth
with straight-falling flames,
a cricket rubs its wings
scraping up a shrill song.

PIGEONS AT REST

The hearts in the pigeons grew cold
and their wings dropped to their sides.

18

ἦρος ἄγγελος ἱμερόφωνος ἀήδων

D 121, E 138, **LP 136**

19

ἀστέρων πάντων ὁ κάλλιστος

D 133, E 32, **LP 104b**

20

ποικίλλεται μὲν γαῖα πολυστέφανος

D 156 (part 1), **E 133**

21

ἔλθοντ' ἐξ ὀράνω πορφυρίαν περθέμενον χλάμυν . . .

D 56, E 69, **LP 54**

THE HERALD

Nightingale, with your
lovely voice you are
the herald of spring.

EVENING STAR

Of all stars Hesperos
is the most beautiful.

CEREMONY

Now the earth with many flowers
puts on her spring embroidery.

DEAR ATTHIS, DID YOU KNOW?

In dream Love came out of heaven
and put on his purple cloak.

22

['Aτθι, σοὶ κἄμ' 'Ανακτορία φίλα]
[πηλόροισ' ἐνὶ] Σάρδε[σιν]
[ναίει, πό]λλακι τυίδε [ν]ῶν ἔχοισα,

ὠς ποτ' ἐζώομεν βίον, ἄς ἔχε
σὲ θέᾳ Fικέλαν ἀρι-
γνώτᾳ, σᾷ δὲ μάλιστ' ἔχαιρε μόλπᾳ.

νῦν δὲ Λύδαισιν ἐμπρέπεται γυναί-
κεσσιν ὡς ποτ' ἀελίω
δύντος ἀ βροδοδάκτυλος σελάννα

πὰρ τὰ περρέχοισ' ἄστρα, φάος δ' ἐπί-
σχει θάλασσαν ἐπ' ἀλμύραν
ἴσως καὶ πολυανθέμοις ἀρούραις,

ἀ δ' ἔερσα κάλα κέχυται τεθά-
λαισι δὲ βρόδα κἄπαλ' ἄν-
θρυσκα καὶ μελίλωτος ἀνθεμώδης.

πόλλα δὲ ζαφοίταισ' ἀγάνας ἐπι-
μνάσθεισ' 'Ατθίδος ἰμμέρῳ,
λέπταν ποι φρένα κῆρ' ἄσᾳ βόρηται.

κῆσί τ' ἔλθην ἄμμ' ὀξυβόη· τὰ δ' οὐ
νῶν γ' ἄπυστα νὺξ πολύω[ς]
γαρύει [πε]ταλόσπο[λ' ὄ]ν τὸ μέσσον.

D 98, **E 86**, LP 96

A LETTER TO ATTHIS I

My Atthis, although our dear Anaktoria
lives in distant Sardis,
she thinks of us constantly, and

of the life we shared in days when for her
you were a splendid goddess,
and your singing gave her deep joy.

Now she shines among Lydian women as
when the red-fingered moon
rises after sunset, erasing

stars around her, and pouring light equally
across the salt sea
and over densely flowered fields;

and lucent dew spreads on the earth to quicken
roses and fragile thyme
and the sweet-blooming honey-lotus.

Now while our darling wanders she remem-
bers lovely Atthis' love,
and longing sinks deep in her breast.

She cries loudly for us to come! We hear,
for the night's many tongues
carry her cry across the sea.

23

. . . Ψάπφ᾽ ἦ μὰν οὔτως ἔγω οὔ σε φιλήσω.
ὦ φαῖν᾽ ἄμμι, κἀξ εὔναν λῦτε τέαν

πεφιλημμ[έν]αν ἴοχυν, ὔδατι δὲ
κρίνον [ὠς ἀ]κήρατον παρὰ κράναν
πέπλον Χῖον ἀπύσχοισα λούεο·

καὶ Κλεῖς σάων καβφέροισα κέδραν
κροκόεντα λώπεά σ᾽ ἐββάλη καὶ
πέπλον πορφύριον· κἀββεβλημένᾳ

χλαίνᾳ πέρ σ᾽ ἐξ[ακ]ρισάντων ἄνθινοι
στέφανοι περ[ὶ σὸν κάρα] δέθεντες,
κἄλθ᾽ ὄσᾳ μαίν[ης μ᾽ ἄδεα καλλ]όνᾳ.

φρῦσσον, ὦ Πρα[ξίνω, κάρ]υ᾽ ἄμμιν, ὠς
παρθένων πό[τον ἀδίω π]οήσω·
ἔκ τινος γὰρ θέων [ταῦτ᾽ ἄ]μμι, τέκνον·

ἦ μὰν τᾷδ᾽ ἀμέρ[ᾳ προτὶ] φιλτάταν
Μυτιλάνναν π[ολίων η]ὔξατ᾽ ἤδη
γυναίκων ἀ κα[λίστα Ψ]άπφ᾽ ἀπύβαν

πεδ᾽ ἀμμέω[ν, ἀ μάτ]ηρ πεδὰ τῶν τέκνων.᾽
φίλια[τ᾽ Ἄτθι, μῶν ἄρα] ταῦτα τὰ πρὶν
ἐπι[λάθεαι πάντ᾽ ἢ] ὀμμναίσᾳ ἔτι; . . .

D 95, E 82, LP 92

A LETTER TO ATTHIS II

[In your own words, Atthis, you said:]
"Sappho, if you do not come out,
I swear, I will love you no more.

O rise and free your lovely strength
from the bed and shine upon us.
Lift off your Chian nightgown, and

like a pure lily by a spring,
bathe in the water. Our Kleïs
will bring a saffron blouse and violet

tunic from your chest. We will place
a clean mantle on you, and crown
your hair with flowers. So come, darling,

with your beauty that maddens us,
and you, Praxinoa, roast the nuts
for our breakfast. One of the gods

is good to us, for on this day
Sappho, most beautiful of women,
will come with us to the white city

of Mytilene, like a mother
among her daughters." Dearest Atthis,
can you now forget all those days?

[Ἀτθιδ᾽ οὔποτ᾽ ἄρ᾽ ὄ]ψ[ομαι,]
τεθνάκην δ᾽ ἀδόλως θέλω.
ἄ με ψισδομένα κατελίππανεν

πόλλα, καὶ τόδ᾽ ἔειπέ μ[οι·]
"Ὤιμ᾽, ὡς δεῖνα πεπ[όνθ]αμεν·
Ψάπφ᾽, ἦ μάν σ᾽ ἀέκοισ᾽ ἀπυλιππάνω.

τὰν δ᾽ ἔγω τάδ᾽ ἀμειβόμαν·
Χαίροισ᾽ ἔρχεο κἄμεθεν
μέμναισ᾽· οἶσθα γὰρ ὥς τε πεδήπομεν.

αἰ δὲ μή, ἀλλά σ᾽ ἔγω θέλω
ὄμναισαι τ[ὰ σ]ὺ [λά]θεαι,
ὄσσ᾽ ἄμμ[ες φίλα] καὶ κάλ᾽ ἐπάσχομεν·

πό[λλοις ἆ στεφάν]οις ἴων
καὶ βρ[όδων γλυ]κίων γ᾽ ὔμοι
κἀπ π[λόκων] πὰρ ἔμοι παρεθήκαο,

καὶ πόλλαις ὑπαθύμιδας
πλέκταις ἀμφ᾽ ἀπάλᾳ δέρᾳ
ἀνθέων ἔκ[ατον] πεποημμέναις,

καὶ πόλλῳ ν[εάρα]ν μύρω[ι]
βρενθείῳ πρ[ὸς ἔμοι χρόα]ν
ἐξαλείψαο κα[ὶ βασ]ιλήιωι,
καὶ στρώμν[αν ἐ]πὶ μολθάκαν
ἀπάλαν πὰρ [ὀπα]υόνων
ἐξίης πόθο[ν ἄβρον Ἰ]ανίδων·
κωὔτε τις [λόφος οὔ]τε τι
ἶρον οὐδ᾽ ὔ[δατος ῥόα]
ἔπλετ᾽ ὄππ[οθεν ἄμ]μες ἀπέσκομεν
οὐκ ἄλσος τ[ί ποτ᾽ εἴ]αρος
[πύκνος ἀρχομένω] ψόφος
[ἀήδων ἔχε ποι]κιλαοιδία,
[ὄττι μὴ σὺν ἔμοι ζαφοί-]
[ταισα] . . .

D 96, E 83, LP 94

TO ATTHIS

So I shall never see Atthis again,
and really I long to be dead,
although she too cried bitterly

when she left, and she said to me,
"Ah, what a nightmare we've suffered.
Sappho, I swear I go unwillingly."

And I answered, "Go, and be happy.
But remember me, for surely you
know how I worshiped you. If not,

then I want to remind you of all
the exquisite days we two shared;
how when near me you would adorn

your hanging locks with violets and
tiny roses and your sapling throat
with necklets of a hundred blossoms;

how your young flesh was rich with kingly
myrrh as you leaned near my breast on
the soft couch where delicate girls

served us all an Ionian could desire;
how we went to every hill, brook,
and holy place, and when early spring

filled the woods with noises of birds
and a choir of nightingales — we two
in solitude were wandering there."

25

Ἔρος δηὖτέ μ᾽ ὁ λυσιμέλης δόνει,
γλυκύπικρον ἀμάχανον ὄρπετον

Ἄτθι, σοὶ δ᾽ ἔμεθεν μὲν ἀπήχθετο
φροντίσδην, ἐπὶ δ᾽ Ἀνδρομέδαν πόται

D 137, E 81, LP 130, 131

26

Ἠράμαν μὲν ἔγω σέθεν, Ἄτθι, πάλαι ποτά,
[ἃς ἔμ᾽ ἀνθεμόεσσ᾽ ἔτι παρθενία σὺ δὲ]
σμίκρα μοι πάϊς ἔμμεν ἐφαίνεο κἄχαρις.

D 40, 41, E 48, LP 49

27

[αἶσ᾽ ἔγων ἔφ]αν Ἄγα[ναι γύναικες,]
[οἶα μ] εμνάσεσθ᾽ ἄ[ϊ μέχρι γῆρας]
[ὄττιν᾽ ἄ]μμες ἐν νεό[ται λάμπρα]
[συνε]πόημμεν·

[ἄγνα μ]ὲν γὰρ καὶ κά[λα πόλλ᾽ ἐν αὖτᾳ]
[δράσα]μεν· πόλι[ν δ᾽ ἀπυλιππανοίσαν]
[σφῶϊν] ὀ[ξ]είαις δ[άκεν ἴμμερός μοι]
[θῦμον ἄσαισι.]

D 34a, E43, LP 24a

TO ATTHIS

Love — bittersweet, irrepressible —
loosens my limbs and I tremble.

Yet, Atthis, you despise my being.
To chase Andromeda, you leave me.

TO ATTHIS

I loved you, Atthis, long ago,
when my girlhood was in full flower
and you were like a graceless child.

LONG DEPARTURE

Then I said to the elegant ladies:
"How you will remember when you are old
the glorious things we did in our youth!

We did many pure and beautiful things.
Now that you are leaving the city,
love's sharp pain encircles my heart."

28

ποικιλόθρον᾽ ἀθανάτ᾽ ᾽Αφρόδιτα,
παῖ Δίος δολόπλοκε, λίσσομαί σε,
μή μ᾽ ἄσαισι μηδ᾽ ὀνίαισι δάμνα,
πότνια, θῦμον,

ἀλλὰ τυίδ᾽ ἔλθ᾽, αἴ ποτα κἀτέρωτα
τὰς ἔμας αὖδας ἀίοισα πήλοι
ἔκλυες, πάτρος δὲ δόμον λίποισα
χρύσιον ἦλθες

ἄρμ᾽ ὑπασδεύξαισα· κάλοι δέ σ᾽ ἆγον
ὤκεες στροῦθοι περὶ γᾶς μελαίνας
πύκνα δίννεντες πτέρ᾽ ἀπ᾽ ὠράνωἴθε-
ρος διὰ μέσσω·

αἶψα δ᾽ ἐξίκο ντο σὺ δ᾽, ὦ μάκαιρα,
μειδιαίσαισ᾽ ἀθανάτωι προσώπωι
ἦρε᾽ ὄττι δηὖτε πέπονθα κὤττι
δηὖτε κάλημμι

κὤττι μοι μάλιστα θέλω γένεσθαι
μαινόλαι θύμωι· τίνα δηὖτε πείθω
ἄψ σάγην ἐς σὰν φιλότατα; τίς σ᾽, ὦ
Ψάπφ᾽, ἀδικήει;

καὶ γὰρ αἰ φεύγει, ταχέως διώξει,
αἰ δὲ δῶρα μὴ δέκετ᾽, ἀλλὰ δώσει,
αἰ δὲ μὴ φίλει, ταχέως φιλήσει
κωὐκ ἐθέλοισα.

ἔλθε μοι καὶ νῦν, χαλέπαν δὲ λῦσον
ἐκ μερίμναν, ὄσσα δέ μοι τέλεσσαι
θῦμος ἰμέρρει, τέλεσον, σὺ δ᾽ αὖτα
σύμμαχος ἔσσο.

D 1, E 1, LP 1, P 1

A PRAYER TO APHRODITE

On your dappled throne, Aphrodite,
sly eternal daughter of Zeus,
I beg you: do not crush me with grief,

but come to me now — as once
you heard my far cry, and yielded,
slipping from your father's house

to yoke the birds to your gold
chariot, and came. Handsome swallows
brought you swiftly to the dark earth,

their wings whipping the middle sky.
Happy, with deathless lips, you smiled:
"What is wrong, why have you called me?

What does your mad heart desire?
Whom shall I make love you, Sappho,
who is turning her back on you?

Let her run away, soon she'll chase you;
refuse your gifts, soon she'll give them.
She will love you, though unwillingly."

Then come to me now and free me
from fearful agony. Labor
for my mad heart, and be my ally.

29

Δεῦρύ μ' ἐκ Κρήτας ἐπ[ὶ τόνδ]ε ναῦον
ἄγνον, ὄππ[αι τοι] χάριεν μὲν ἄλσος
μαλί[αν], βῶμοι δὲ τεθυμιάμε-
νοι [λι]βανώτωι·

ἐν δ' ὕδωρ ψῦχρον κελάδει δι' ὔσδων
μαλίνων, βρόδοισι δὲ παῖς ὁ χῶρος
ἐσκίαστ', αἰθυσσομένων δὲ φύλλων
κῶμα κατέρρει·

ἐν δὲ λείμων ἱππόβοτος τέθαλεν
ἠείνοισιν ἄνθεσιν, ἔν δ' ἄηται
μέλλιχα πνέοισιν [
                        ]

ἔνθα δὴ σὺ στέμματ' ἔλοισα, Κύπρι
χρυσίαισιν ἐν κυλίκεσσιν ἄβρως
ὀμμεμείχμενον θαλίαισι νέκταρ
οἰνοχόαισον.

B 196, D 516, D Suppl. p. 30, E 4, 6, LP 2

TO APHRODITE OF THE FLOWERS, AT KNOSSOS

Leave Crete and come to this holy temple
where the pleasant grove of apple trees
circles an altar smoking with frank-
    incense.

Here roses leave shadow on the ground
and cold springs babble through apple branches
where shuddering leaves pour down pro-
    found sleep.

In our meadow where horses graze
and wild flowers of spring blossom,
anise shoots fill the air with a-
    roma.

And here, Queen Aphrodite, pour
heavenly nectar into gold cups
and fill them gracefully with sud-
    den joy.

30

Πλάσιον δή μ' [εὐχομέναι φανείη,]
πότνι' Ἤρα, σὰ χ[αρίεσσα μόρφα,
τὰν ἀράταν Ἀτ[ρεῖδαι . . . κλῆ-]
τοι βασίληες·

ἐκτελέσσαντες μ[άλα πόλλ' ἄεθλα,]
πρῶτα μὲν πὲρ Ἴ[λιον, ἔν τε πόντωι]
τυίδ' ἀπορμάθε[ντες, ὅδον περαίνην]
οὐκ ἐδύναντο,

πρὶν σὲ καὶ Δί' ἀντ[ίαον κάλεσσαι]
καὶ Θυώνας ἰμε[ρόεντα παῖδα·]
νῦν δὲ κ[ἄμοι πραϋμένης ἄρηξον]
κὰτ τὸ πάλαιον· . . .

D 28, E 40, LP 17, **P 17**

31

γλύκηα μᾶτερ, οὔτοι δύναμαι κρέκην τὸν ἴστον
πόθωι δάμεισα παῖδος βραδίναν δι' Ἀφροδίταν

D 114, E 135, **LP 102**

TO LADY HERA

Lady Hera, while I pray let your
graceful form appear, which came once
to the dazzling kings, the Atreidai,
when they prayed.

The Atreidai accomplished many feats
first at Ilium, and then on the sea
on their voyage here, but could not
reach home again

before imploring you, Zeus of the winds
and Thyone's lovely child: Dionysos.
So be kind, as in former days,
and now help *me*.

PARALYSIS

Mother darling, I cannot work the loom
for sweet Kypris has almost crushed me,
broken me with love for a slender boy.

32

δολοπλόκας γὰρ Κυπρογένεος πρόπολον

D 156, **E 134**

33

[ʾΩ Ψάπφοι], σύ τε κἆμος θεράπων ʾʾΕρος

D 110, **E 75**, LP 159

34

φίλτατον Γαίας γένος ʾΟρράνω τε

E 31, LP 198

DESIRE

For I am
a slave of the Kypros-born,
who lays a net of trickery.

FROM APHRODITE

I tell you, Sappho,
love is my servant.

TO EROS

From all the offspring
of the earth and heaven
love is the most precious.

35

καιθνα[ί]σκει, Κυθέρη᾽, ἄβρος ᾽Άδωνις· τί κε θεῖμεν;
καιτύπτεσθε, κόραι, καὶ κατερείκεσθε κίθωνας.

D 107, E 103, **LP 140**

36

χερρόμακτρα δὲ κὰγ γενύων
πορφύρα καταρτιαμένα, τὰ Τῖμας
εῖς [τ᾽] ἔπεμψ᾽ ἀπὺ Φωκάας,
δῶρα τίμια

D 99, **E 87**, LP 101

37

ζὰ . . . ἐλεξάμαν ὄναρ Κυπρογένηα

D 87, E 123, **LP 134**

THE DEATH OF ADONIS

Our tender Adonis is dying, O Kythereia,
What can we do?
Beat on your breasts, my girls, and tear
your dresses.

LOVE TOKEN

Your face is shaded, Aphrodite,
with a kerchief of porphyry
color: a precious gift from Timas
of far Phokaia.

DIALOGUE

Kypros-born, in dream
we two were talking.

38

σοὶ δ᾽ ἔγω λεύκας ἐπὶ δᾶμον αἶγος
[πίονα καύσω],

κἀπιλείψω τοι

D 8, **E 7, 8**, LP 40

39

αἴθ᾽ ἔγω, χρυσοστέφαν᾽ Ἀφρόδιτα,
τόνδε τὸν πάλον λαχοίην

D 9, E 9, **LP 33**

40

χρυσόφανες ὦ Ϝεκάτα θεράπνα
Ἀφροδίτας

D 145, **E 24**, LP Incert. 23

TO APHRODITE

For you, Aphrodite, I will burn
the savory fat of a white she-goat.
All this I will leave behind for you.

TO APHRODITE

Aphrodite with gold flowers in your hair,
I say if only
some other fate were mine!

HEKATE

Hekate, shining of gold,
handmaid to Aphrodite.

41

ῶ γένος θελξίμβροτον 'Αφροδίτας

E 33, LP 200

42

βροδοπάχεες ἄγναι Χάριτες δεῦτε Δίος κόραι

D 57, E 68, LP 53

43

δεῦτέ νυν ἄβραι Χάριτες καλλίκομοί τε Μοῖσαι

D 90, E 101, LP 128

PEITHO (PERSUASION)

You are the daughter of Aphrodite:
you confuse us
and we mortals love.

TO THE GRACES

O daughters of Zeus,
come to me now,
O Graces of the pink arms.

TO THE GRACES AND MUSES

Come, come now,
tender Graces,
and Muses of the splendid hair.

44

δεῦρο δηὖτε, Μοῖσαι, χρύσιον λίποισαι
[δῶμα]

D 154, **E 129**, LP 127

45

αἲ με τιμίαν ἐπόησαν ἔργα
τὰ σφὰ δοῖσαι

D 10, E 10, **LP 32**

46

δαύοις ἀπάλας ἐτάρας ἐν στήθεσιν

D 134, E 128, **LP 126**

MAKING OF THE POEM

Come to me now, Muses.
Leave your gold house.

THE MUSES

To me they brought honor, for they
gave me the secret of their craft.

SLEEP

May you find sleep on a
soft girlfriend's breast.

47

Ψάπφοι, τί τὰν πολύολβον ᾿Αφροδίταν
[ἀτίμασας]

D 144b, **E 126,** LP 133 (16A)

48

μάλα δὴ κεκορημένοις
Γόργως

D 143, E 55, **LP 144**

49

οἷον τὸ γλυκύμαλον ἐρεύθεται ἄκρωι ἐπ᾿ ὔσδωι,
ἄκρον ἐπ᾿ ἀκροτάτωι, λελάθοντο δὲ μαλοδρόπηες,
οὐ μὰν ἐκλελάθοντ᾿, ἀλλ᾿ οὐκ ἐδύναντ᾿ ἐπίκεσθαι

οἴαν τὰν ὑάκινθον ἐν ὤρεσι ποίμενες ἄνδρες
πόσσι καταστείβοισι, χάμαι δέ τε πόρφυρον ἄνθος

D 116, 117, E 150, 151, **LP 105a, c**

BECAUSE OF A RIVAL

Sappho, why do you condemn
the many joys of Aphrodite?

A RIVAL

By now they've had
their fill of Gorgo.

THE VIRGIN

Like a sweet apple reddening on the high
tip of the topmost branch and forgotten
by the pickers — no, beyond their reach.

Like a hyacinth crushed in the mountains
by shepherds; lying trampled on the earth
yet blooming purple.

50

παρθένοισι
μελλιχοφώναις

E 30, LP 185

51

αἲ τ᾽ ὄρααι στεφαναπλόκην

D 101, **E 67,** LP 125

52

τίωισ᾽ ὦ φίλε γάμβρε, κάλως ἐικάσδω;
ὄρπακι βραδίνωι σε πάλιστ᾽ ἐικάσδω.

D 127, E 161, **LP 115**

SAPPHO'S EPITHET

> The honey-voiced virgins.

LOOPS OF FLOWERS

Girls ripe for marriage
were braiding flowers.

BRIDEGROOM

What are you, my lovely bridegroom?
You are most like a slender sapling.

53

πάρθενοι δ[. . .
παννυχίσδ[οισ]α[ι] . . .
σὰν ἀείδοιεν φ[ιλότατα καὶ νύμ-]
φας ἰοκόλπω,

ἀλλ' ἐγέρθεις ἠιθ[έοις] . . .
στεῖχε σοῖς ὑμάλικ[ας, ὤς κ' ἐλάσσω]
ἤπερ ὄσσον ἀ λιγύφω[νος ὄρνις]
ὔπνον [ἴ]δωμεν

B, p. 221, D 39, E 47, LP 30

54

ἀλλ' ἄγιτ', ὦ φίλαι,
[ἀοίδας ἀπυλήξομεν], ἄγχι γὰρ ἀμέρα

D 54, **E 65,** LP 43

WEDDING SONG

Groom, we virgins at your door
will pass the night singing of the love
between you and your bride. Her breasts
are like violets.

Wake and call out the young men
your friends, and you can walk the streets
and we shall sleep less tonight than
the bright nightingale.

TO HER FRIENDS AT DAWN

Come, my darling girls,
let us stop singing now
for soon it will be day.

55

[Νύμφα ροδέων ἐρώτων βρύουσα, νύμφα Παφίης
ἄγαλμα κάλλιστον, ἴθι πρὸς εὐνήν, ἴθι πρὸς λέχος,
μείλιχα παίζουσα, γλυκεῖα νυμφίῳ. Ἕσπερός σ᾽ ἑκοῦσαν
ἄγοι, ἀργυρόθρονον ζυγίαν Ἥραν θαυμάζουσαν.]*

E 147

56

οὐ γὰρ ἑτέρα νῦν πάις ὦ γάμβρε τεαύτα

D 130, E 163, **LP 113**

* Prose paraphrase by Edmonds from Himerius *Epithalamy
of Severus.* — Ed.

SONG OF THE WEDDING BED

Bride, warm with rose-
colored love, brightest
ornament of the Paphian,
come to the bedroom now,
enter the bed and play
tenderly with your man.
May the Evening Star
lead you eagerly
to that instant when you
will gaze in wonder
before the silver throne
of Hera, queen of marriage.

SONG FOR THE BRIDE

No girl who ever was,
O groom, was like her.

57

ὄλβιε γάμβρε, σοὶ μὲν δὴ γάμος, ὡς ἄραο
ἐκτετέλεστ', ἔχεις δὲ πάρθενον, ἂν ἄραο·

μελλίχιος δ' ἐπ' ἱμμέρτῳ κέχυται προσώπῳ

σοὶ χάριεν μὲν εἶδος
κὤππατα μελλιχόχροα
[νύμφ',] ἔρος δὲ [τέῳ] κάλῳ
περκέχυται προσώπῳ,

καί σε τέτικεν ἐξόχως
Ἀφρόδιτα

D 128, E 155, 156, 158, LP 112

58

ἴψοι δὴ τὸ μέλαθρον·
   ὑμήναον·
ἀέρρετε τέκτονες ἄνδρες·
   ὑμήναον.
γάμβρος εἰσέρχεται ἴσος Ἄρευι,
ἄνδρος μεγάλω πόλυ μέζων.

D 123, E 148, LP 111

AFTER THE CEREMONY

Happy groom, the wedding took place
and the girl you prayed for is yours.

Now her charming face is warm with love.

My bride, your body is a joy,
your eyes as soft as honey,
and love pours its light
on your perfect features.

Using all her skill Aphrodite
honored you.

A LANKY GROOM

Raise the ceiling and sing
Hymen!
Have carpenters raise the roof.
Hymen!
The groom who will come in
is tall like towering Ares.

59

κῆ δ᾽ ἀμβροσίας μὲν
κράτηρ ἐκέκρατ᾽
Ἔρμαις δ᾽ ἔλων ὄλπιν θέοισ᾽ ὠινοχόαισε.
κῆνοι δ᾽ ἄρα πάντες
καρχάσι᾽ ἦχον
κἄλειβον ἀράσαντο δὲ πάμπαν ἔσλα
τῶι γάμβρωι.

D 135, 136, E 146, **LP 141**

60

χαῖρε, νύμφα, χαῖρε, τίμιε γάμβρε, πόλλα

χαίροις ἀ νύμφα, χαιρέτω δ᾽ ὁ γάμβρος

D 128, 129, E 160, 162, **LP 116, 117**

61

θυρώρωι πόδες ἐπτερόγυιοι,
τὰ δὲ σάμβαλα πεμπεβόηα,
πίσυγγοι δὲ δέκ᾽ ἐξεπόναισαν

D 124, E 154, **LP 110**

DRINKS FOR THE GROOM

The wine bowl was full
with perfect ambrosia.
Hermes took up a jug to pour wine for the gods;
then all gripped their goblets,
spilled out libations,
and shouted lots of good luck
to the groom.

GOODBY, BE HAPPY

Goodby, be happy, bride and groom.

Be happy, bride and honored groom.

THE GUARD OUTSIDE THE BRIDAL CHAMBER

The doorkeeper's feet are fourteen
yards long. Ten shoemakers used up
five oxhides to cobble each sandal.

62

οὐκ οἶδ᾽ ὄττι θέω· δίχα μοι τὰ νοήμματα

D 46, E 52, **LP 51**

63

τοῦτο δ᾽ ἴσθι, διπλασίαν
κήναν νύκτ᾽ ἄρασθαί μ᾽ ἄμμι γένεσθαι

E 84A, LP 197

64

πλήρης μὲν ἐφαίνετ᾽ ἀ σελάννα
αἰ δ᾽ ὡς περὶ βῶμον ἐστάθησαν

Κρῆσσαί νύ ποτ᾽ ὦδ᾽ ἐμμελέως πόδεσσιν
ὄρχηντ᾽ ἀπάλοις᾽ ἀμφ᾽ ἐρόεντα βῶμον
πόας τέρεν ἄνθος μάλακον μάτεισαι

D 88, 93, E 112, 114, **LP 154, Incert. 16**

SHALL I?

I do not know what to do:
I say yes — and then no.

ONE NIGHT

All the while, believe me, I prayed
our night would last twice as long.

DANCERS

While the full moon rose, young girls
took their place around the altar.

In old days Cretan girls danced
supplely around an altar of love,
crushing the soft flowering grass.

65

Ὦ κάλ', ὦ χαρίεσσα, σοὶ
αἰ βροδόσφυροι Χάριτες
χρύσια τ' Ἀφρόδιτα
συμπαίζοισι

E 157

66

παρθενία, παρθενία, ποῖ με λίποισα οἴχηι;
οὐκέτι ἤξω πρὸς σέ, οὐκέτι ἤξω.

D 131, E 164, **LP 114**

67

ἦρ' ἔτι παρθενίας ἐπιβάλλομαι;

D 53, E 159, **LP 107**, P 53

BRIDE

O beautiful, O charming bride,
now you play with gold Aphrodite
and the roseate-ankled
Graces.

LOSS

Virginity, virginity, when you leave me,
where do you go?

I am gone and never come back to you.
I never return.

REMORSE

Do I still long
for my virginity?

Κύπρο . . .

κᾶρυξ ἦλθ[ε] θό[ων δυνάμι μ]ελέ[ων] ἔθεις
Ἰδάοις τάδε κ[ᾶ]λα φ[όρ]εις τάχυς ἄγγελος
. . . .
τάς τ' ἄλλας Ἀσίας τ[ά]δ' ἔλον κλέος ἄφθιτον.
'Ἔκτωρ καὶ συνέταιροι ἄγοισ' ἐλικώπιδα
Θήβας ἐξ ἰάρας Πλακίας τ' ἀπ' ἐννάω
ἄβραν Ἀνδρομάχαν ἐνὶ ναῦσιν ἐπ' ἄλμυρον
πόντον· πόλλα δ' [ἐλί]γματα χρύσια κάμματα
πορφύρ[α] κἀν ἀύτμενα ποίκιλ' ἀθρήματα,
ἀργύρ[α τ'] ἀνάριθμα ποτήρια κἀλέφαις.'
ὢς εἶπ'· ὀτραλέως δ' ὀνόρουσε πάτ[ηρ] φίλος,
φάμα δ' ἦλθε κατὰ πτόλιν εὐρύχορον Fίλω.
αὔτικ' Ἰλιάδαι σατίναις ὐπ' ἐϋτρόχοις
ἆγον αἰμιόνοις, ἐπέβαινε δὲ παῖς ὄχλος
γυναίκων τ' ἄμα παρθενίκαν τ' ἀπ[αλ]οσφύρων
χῶρις δ' αὖ Περάμοιο θύγαιρες [ἐπήισαν.]
ἴππ[οις] δ' ἄνδρες ὔπαγον ὐπ' ἄρ[ματα, σὺν δ' ἴσαν]
π[άντες] ἀΐθεοι· μεγάλωστι δ' ἴεν μέγας]
δ[ᾶμος] κἀνίοχοι φ[αλάροισ]ι [κεκαδμέναις]
π[ώλοις ἔ]ξαγο[ν.] . . .
. . . .
[ὄτα δεῦτ' ὀχέων ἐπέβαν ἴ]κελοι θέοι[ς]
[Ἔκτωρ Ἀνδρομάχα τε, σύν]αγνον ἀόλ[λεες]
ὄρμα τ' ἀ π[όλις ἄψ ἐράτει]νον ἐς Ἴλιο[ν]
αὖλος δ' ἀδυμέλη[ς κιθάρα] τ' ὀνεμείχνυ[το]
καὶ ψόφος κροτάλ[ων λιγέ]ως δ' ἄρα πάρ[θενοι]
ἄειδον μέλος ἄγν[ον, ἴκα]νε δ' ἐς αἴθ[ερα]
ἄχω θεσπεσία γέλ[ασαν δὲ τ'] Ὀλύμπιοι·
πάντα δ' ἦς κατ' ὄδο[ις θαλία· κεκέραντο γάρ]
κράτηρες φίαλαί τ' ἐπ[ί τ' ε]ϋεδέ[ω]ν πλάκ[ω]ν
μύρρα καὶ κασία λίβανός τ' ὀνελίχνυτο·
γύναικες δ' ἐλέλυσδον ὄσαι προγενέστεραι,
πάντες δ' ἄνδρες ἐπήρατον ἴαχον ὄρθιον
πάον' ὀγκαλέοντες ἐκάβολον εὐλύραν,
ὔμνην δ' Ἔκτορα κ' Ἀνδρομάχαν θεοεικέλο[ις.]

D 55a, b, E 66, LP 44

WEDDING OF ANDROMACHE

Kypros.
A herald came, racing powerfully on swift legs,
came quickly to the people of Ida with tidings

of imperishable renown in the rest of Asia:
"Hektor and his comrades bring a dark-eyed girl
from holy Thebe and the streams of Plakia;
splendid Andromache coming with the navy
over the salt sea. They bear many gold bracelets
and purple gowns and odd trinkets of rare design
and countless silver goblets and pieces of ivory."

So the herald spoke; and Priam sprang to his feet
and the glowing news was carried to his friends
throughout the wide city. Instantly the sons of Ilios
harnessed the mules to the finely-wheeled chariots,
and a throng of wives and slender-ankled virgins
climbed inside. Priam's daughters rode alone,
while young men led their horses under the carts
and drove them out of the city . . .

Like gods . . . holy . . . they all set out for Ilium
to the confusion of sweet flutes and crashing
        cymbals,
and the virgins sang a loud heavenly song
whose wonderful echo touched the sky. Everywhere
was laughter in the streets and bowls and chalices.

Myrrh and cassia and incense rode on the wind.
Elder women shouted and all the men sang out
with thrilling power and raised a paean to Apollo —
O mighty bowman and skillful player of the lyre —
singing of Hektor and Andromache as of gods.

69

Θῦμ[ε,] ϱ[ᾷσ]ον· οὐ[κ] ἄ[μ]μι θέαισι μόρφαν ἐπί[με]ϱον ἐξίης
θόαισ᾽ ὐ[μν]οχέταισ᾽ [᾽Αδ]ωνίδηον

[φϱοντίδεσσιν· ἀλλ᾽ ἄ]στο[μον γ]ὰϱ ἀτι-
μόμ[βϱοτ]ο[ς ἴσσε τ᾽] ῎Ιμεϱος
καὶ δαμ[ασσικάϱδι]ος ᾽Αφϱοδίτα,

κὰδ δὲ μ[έλλιχον νέκταϱ ἔχευ᾽ ἀπὺ
χϱυσίας [φϱενω]λοία
[πϱο]χ[όω τέαις πϱαπίδ]εσσι Πείθω.

D 98 (ll. 21-29), E 86A(App.), LP 96 (ll. 21-29)

70

῎Ηλθες· κεῦ ἐποίησας· ἔγω δέ σε
μάόμαν, ὂν δ᾽ ἔφλαξας ἔμαν φϱένα
καυομέναν πόθῳ· χαῖϱ᾽ ἄμμι, [χαῖϱε]

πόλλα καὶ Fισάϱιθμα τόσῳ χϱόνῳ
ἀλλάλαν ἀπελείφθημεν.

D 48, E 89, LP 48

TO HERSELF

Let the depths of my soul be dumb
for I cannot think up
a clarion song about Adonis,

for Aphrodite who staggers me
with shameful lust
has reduced me to dull silence,

and Persuasion (who maddens one)
from her gold vial
spills tangy nectar on my mind.

HOMECOMING

You came. And you did well to come.
I longed for you and you brought fire
to my heart, which burns high for you.

Welcome, darling, be blessed three times
for all the hours of our separation.

71

πόλλα μοι τὰν Πωλυανάκτιδα παῖδα χαίρην

D 150, E 121, LP 155

72

ἔχει μὲν ᾿Ανδρομέδα κάλαν ἀμοίβαν . . .

D 144a, E 125, LP 133(16)

73

τίς δ᾿ ἀγροίωτις θέλγει νόον . . .
ἀγροίωτιν ἐπεμμένα σπόλαν . . .
οὐκ ἐπισταμένα τὰ βράκε᾿ ἔλκην ἐπὶ τῶν σφύρων;

D 61, E 98, LP 57

74

ἀλλ᾿ ὂν μὴ μεγαλύννεο δακτυλίω πέρι

D 45, E 51, LP Incert. 5

HER RIVAL'S PEDIGREE

A bright good morning,
Andromeda — O daughter
from kings and sons of kings.

RIVAL

I have lost, and you, Andromeda,
have made an excellent exchange.

ANDROMEDA, WHAT NOW?

Can this farm girl
in farm-girl finery burn your heart?
She is even ignorant of the way
to lift her gown over her ankles.

A RING

Silly woman. Yes, it is a ring,
but really, don't be so proud.

75

Ἥρων ἐξεδίδαξε Γυάρων τὰν ἀννόδρομον

E 62, E 73, **LP Incert. 11**

76

ὁ δ᾽ Ἄρευς φαῖσί κεν Ἄφαιστον ἄγην βίᾳ.

D Alc. 9a, **E 70**, LP Alc. 349b

77

Λάτω καὶ Νιόβα μάλα μὲν φίλαι ἦσαν ἔταιραι

D 119, E 140, **LP 142**

78

τί με Πανδίονις ὤρρανα χελίδω

D 86, **E 122**, LP 135

THE GIRL-RUNNER HERO

I taught Hero from the island
of Gyara
how to run like a star.

ARES' STRENGTH

Ares lets everybody
know that he could
drag off Hephaistos
with his bare hands.

BEFORE THE MURDER

It seems untrue but
once Leto and Niobe
were devoted friends.

TO THE NIGHTINGALE'S SISTER

Why do you trouble me — Pandion's
daughter, swallow out of heaven?

79

ὁ πλοῦτος [δ'] ἄνευ ἀρέτας
οὐκ ἀσίνης πάροικος·
ἀ δ' ἐξ ἀμφοτέρων κρᾶσις
δαιμονίαν ἄκραν ἔχει

D 92, **E 100,** LP 148

80

καιθάνοισα δὲ κείσηι οὐδέ ποτα μναμοσύνα σέθεν
ἔσσετ' οὐδὲ ποκ' ὕστερον· οὐ γὰρ πεδέχηις βρόδων
τὼν ἐκ Πιερίας· ἀλλ' ἀφάνης κἀν 'Αίδα δόμωι
φοιτάσηις πεδ' ἀμαύρων νεκύων ἐκπεποταμένα.

D 58, E 71, **LP 55**

81

ὄσταθι κἄντα [θᾶ με φίλαν] φίλος
καὶ τὰν ἐπ' ὄσσοισ' ὀμπέτασον χάριν.

D 151, **E 120,** LP 138

MONEY AND VIRTUE

If you are rich but not good
you court calamity,
yet being both
                you stand
at the happy top of the world.

TO AN UNEDUCATED WOMAN

When dead you will lie forever forgotten,
for you have no claim to the Pierian roses.
Dim here, you will move more dimly in Hell,
flitting among the undistinguished dead.

TO A HANDSOME MAN

Stand up and gaze on me as friend
to friend. I ask you to reveal
the naked beauty of your eyes.

82

Ἰόπλοκ᾽ ἄγνα μελλιχόμειδε Σάπφοι,
θέλω τι Ϝείπην ἀλλά με κωλύει αἴδως.

αἰ δ᾽ ἦχες ἔσλων ἴμμερον ἢ κάλων
καὶ μή τι Ϝείπην γλῶσσ᾽ ἐκύκα κάκον,
αἴδως κεν οὐκί σ᾽ ἦχεν ὄππατ᾽,
ἀλλ᾽ ἔλεγες περὶ τῶ δικαίως.

D Alc. 63, Sa. 149, **E Alc. 124, Sa. 119,** LP Alc. 384, Sa. 137

83

ὁ μὲν γὰρ κάλος ὄσσον ἴδην πέλεται [κάλος],
ὁ δὲ κἄγαθος αὔτικα καὶ κάλος ἔσσεται.

D 49, E 58, **LP 50**

CONVERSATION WITH ALKAIOS

Alkaios
Violet-haired, pure, honey-smiling Sappho,
I want to speak to you but shame disarms me.

Sappho
If you cared for what is upright and good,
and your tongue were not concocting trouble,
shame would not be hiding in your eyes
and you would speak out your real desires.

APPEARANCES

A handsome man now looks handsome.
A good man will soon take on beauty.

84

[Τ]ὰν τ[αχίσταν, ὦ κ]έλομαί σ᾽, ὄ[νελθε,]
[Γό]γγυλα β[ρόδ]ανθι, λάβοισα μάν[δυν]
[γλα]κρίναν· σε δηῦτε πόθος τι[ς ἄμος]
ἀμφιπόταται

τὰν κάλαν· ἀ γὰρ κατάγωγις αὔτα
ἐπτόαισ᾽ ἴδοισαν, ἔγω δὲ χαίρω.
καὶ γὰρ αὔτα δή π[οτ᾽] ἐμεμ[φόμαν τὰν]
[Κ]υπρογέν[ηαν·]

[τ]ᾶς ἄραμα[ι μὴ χάριν ἀβφέρην μοι]
τοῦτο τῶ[πος, ἀλλά σε, τὰν μάλιστα]
[β]όλλομα[ι θνάταν κατίδην γυναίκων]
[ἄψ πάλιν ἔλκην.]

D 36, E 45, LP 22

85

καὶ ποθήω καὶ μάομαι . . .

D 20, E 23, LP 36

RETURN

O Gongyla, my darling rose,
put on your milk-white gown. I want
you to come back quickly. For my
desire feeds on

your beauty. Each time I see your gown
I am made weak and happy. I too
blamed the Kyprian. Now I pray
she will not seek

revenge, but may she soon allow
you, Gongyla, to come to me
again: you whom of all women
I most desire.

UNGIVEN LOVE

I am dry with longing
and I hunger for her.

86

[ἐν θυέλλαισι ζαφ]έλοισι ναῦται
[ἐκφοβήθεντες] μεγάλαις ἀήται[ς]
[ἄββαλον τὰ φόρτι]α κἀπὶ χέρσω
[πλοῖον ὄκελλαν·]

[μὴ μάλιστ᾽ ἔγωγ᾽ ἀ]᾽μοθεν πλέοιμ[ι]
[χειμάσαντος, μη]δὲ τὰ φόρτι᾽ εἶκ[α]
[ἀββάλην εἰς ἄλμα]ν ἄτιμ᾽, ἐπεὶ κῆ-
[τ᾽ ἐν φρέσι τάρβος·]

[αἰ δε Νήρηι προ]ρέοντι πόμπᾳ
[ἐννάλῳ τἀμ᾽ ἐξέσει]αι δέκε[σθαι]
[φόρτι᾽] . . .

D 31, **E 41**, LP 20

87

οὐδ᾽ ἴαν δοκίμωμι προσίδοισαν φάος ἀλίω
ἔσσεσθαι σοφίαν πάρθενον εἰς οὐδένα πω χρόνον
τεαύταν

D 60, E 72, **LP 56**

IN TIME OF STORM

When sea-storms scream across the water,
the sailor, fearing these wild blasts,
spills his cargo overboard and veers
                  his vessel shoreward.

I pray that I may be bound nowhere
in time of storm, yet let my heart
not cast her cargo fearfully
                  into the salt depths,

but let Nereus, with all the proper
ocean ceremonies, receive
                  the gift of my goods.

ART

No girl I think will ever outshine
your skill — no girl who will ever
look into sunlight.

88

Διὸς γὰρ πάις ἐστ᾽ ὀ χρύσος·
κῆνον οὐ σέες οὐδὲ κῖς
δαρδάπτοισ᾽· ὀ δὲ δάμναται
καὶ φρένων βροτέαν κράτιστον.

E 110, LP 204

89

. . . πόδας δὲ
ποίκιλος μάσλης ἐκάλυπτε, Λύδι-
ον κάλον ἔργον.

D 17, E 20, LP 39

90

ἀμφὶ δ᾽ ἄβροισ᾽ . . . λασίοισ᾽ εὖ ἐπύκασσε

D 85, E 105, LP 100

A CHILD OF GOD

Gold is a child of God.
Moths and worms
do not eat it.
                    Gold overpowers
a man's heart,
even of the strongest man.

ASIAN DYES

Her gay embroidered gown
draped down to her toes:
fine needlework from Lydia.

ON AMORGINE FABRICS

She wore around her the soft
fine linen robes of Amorgos.

91

παντοδάπαισι μεμειχμένα χροίαισιν

D 142, E 21, **LP 152**

92

ἔγω δ᾽ ἐπὶ μολθάκαν
τύλαν κασπολέω μέλεα· κᾶν μὲν τε τύλαγκας ἀσπόλεα

D 42, E 56, 57, **LP 46**

93

ἰάνω μαλακωτέρα

χρύσω χρυσοτέρα

πόλυ πάκτιδος ἀδυμελεστέρα

ὠίω πόλυ λευκότερον

D 138, 139, **E 61, 60, 59, 62,** LP 156, 167

JASON'S CLOTHING

His cloak was of a cloth
handspun from many colors.

WHEN YOU COME

You will lie down and
I shall lay out soft
pillows for your body.

COMPARISONS

Softer than fine robes.

More golden than gold.

Sweeter than the lyre.

Far whiter than an egg.

94

πέρροχος, ὡς ὅτ' ἄοιδος ὁ Λέσβιος ἀλλοδάποισιν

D 115, E 148 (ll. 9-11), LP 106

95

σὺ δὲ στεφάνοις, ὦ Δίκα, πέρθεσθ' ἐράτοις φόβαισιν
ὄρπακας ἀνήτω συναέρραισ' ἀπάλαισι χέρσιν·
εὐάνθεα γὰρ πέλεται καὶ Χάριτες μάκαιραι
μᾶλλον προτερην, ἀστεφανώτοισι δ' ἀπυστρέφονται.

D 80, E 117, LP 81, b

96

εὐμορφοτέρα Μνασιδίκα τὰς ἀπάλας Γυρίννως

D 63, E 115, LP 82a

THE PRE-EMINENCE OF LESBIAN POETRY

Towering over all lands
is the singer of Lesbos.

TO DIKA, NOT TO GO BAREHEADED

Dika, take some shoots of dill, and loop
them skillfully about your lovely hair.
The happy Graces love her who wears flowers
but turn their back on one who goes plain.

THE BEAUTY OF HER GIRLS

Mnasidika has a lovelier body
than even our soft Gyrinno's.

97

ἀλλά, μὴ κάμπιε στέραν φρένα

D 141, E 93, LP Incert. 5, l. 2

98

σκιδναμένας ἐν στήθεσιν ὄργας
πεφύλαχθαι γλῶσσαν μαψυλάκαν

D 126, E 137, LP 158

99

θέοι δ[αίμ]ονες ὦρ[ον ἐπα]ύτικα δάκ[ρυα]

D 156B, E 50A(App.), LP 139

100

γάνος ζάφθερρον τὰς ὄψ-
ις ὑακινθίνῳ ἄνθεῖ ὅμοιον.

E 90, LP 196, R 122

YIELDING

No more. Do not try
to bend a hard heart.

TRIAL

When anger floods into my chest,
I bite my tongue — not to explode.

BECAUSE OF THE PUNISHMENT

Tears came to the eyes
of even the holy gods.

A VISION OF MYTILENE

Like the hyacinth
there is a light
blinding my eyes.

101

ὡς δὲ πάις πεδὰ μάτερα πεπτερύγωμαι

D 51, E 142, **LP Incert. 25**

102

ἢ τίν' ἄλλον
[μᾶλλον] ἀνθρώπων ἔμεθεν φίλησθα;

D 18, **E 22**, LP 129, 1. 2

103

ὥς τε, μέλημα τῶμον,
περπτύγω

D 147, **E 29**, LP 163

104

τὸν δ' ἐπιπλάζοντ' ἄνοαι φέροιεν
καὶ μελέδωναι

D 14, **E 18**, LP 37

A RETURN

Safe now. I've flown to you
like a child to its mother.

OUT OF ALL MANKIND

Is there in any land
any man whom you love
more than you love me?

I WOULD FLY TO THE VERY FOOT OF YOUR MOUNTAINS

I would go anywhere
to take you in my arms
again, my darling.

TO HER DETRACTOR

As for him who blames me,
let him walk with madness
and stumble through sorrows.

105

Εὔιδόν ποτ᾽ ἄνθε᾽ ἀμέρ-
γοισαν παῖδ᾽ ἄγαν ἀπάλαν ἔγω

D 111, E 107, LP 122

106

ἄβρα, δηὖτέ [σε] πάγχη ἄς πάλαι ἀλλόμαν

D 140, E 96, LP Incert. 5, l. 3

107

. . . [ὄ]ττινα[ς γὰρ] . . .
[εὖ θέω, κῆνοί με μά]λιστα πά[ντων] . . .
. . . [σίνοντα]ι . . .

D 37, E 13, LP 26, ll. 2-4

108

μήτε μοι μέλι μήτε μέλισσα

D 52, E 106, LP 146

A GIRL

One day I watched a tender girl
picking some wild flowers.

HOMECOMING

Soft girl from whom I was
altogether cut off,
I have come home again.

WEATHERCOCKS

Those whom I treated kindly,
especially injure me now.

HAVING REFUSED TO ACCEPT
THE BITTER WITH THE SWEET

I will never find again
honey or the honey bee.

109

ὅτα πάννυχος ἄσφι κατάγρει
[ὅππατ' ἄωρος]

ὀφθάλμοις δὲ μέλαις χύτο νύκτος ἄωρος

D 125, 106, **E 141, 141A,** LP 149, 151

110

. . . καὶ γὰρ δὴ σύ [μ' ἴες] προτ[' οἶκον]
[ἄρτ]ι κἤσμελπες· κ[ατὰ] ταῦτα [δ' ἤκω.]
[ὦ] ζάλεξαι· κὰ[δ δ' ἴθι], τὼ δὲ κ[άλλεος]
[ἄ]δρα χάριοσα[ι·]

[σ]τείχομεν γὰρ [πλάσι]ον· εὖ δὲ [Ϝοῖσθα]
[κα]ὶ σὺ τοῦτ'· ἀλλ' [ὅττι] τάχιστα [ταῖς σαις]
[πα]ρ[θ]ένοις ἄπ[π]εμπε· θέοι [δὲ δῷέν]
[μ' ὦ κ]εν ἔχοιεν.

D 38, **E 46,** LP 27

REST

The night closed their eyes
and then night poured down
black sleep upon their lids.

AN ENCOUNTER

You came to my house and sang to me,
and so I have come. Speak. Come down
and release me from the silence of
your beauty.

We were walking near your home when you
saw us. Now I ask: quickly, send your
girls away, and may the gods grant me
what they will.

111

[ὄττα γὰρ κ᾽ ἐνάν]τιον εἰσίδω σ[ε]
[τόττ᾽ ἔμοι οὐ φύνν᾽] ᾽Ερμιόνα τεαύ[τα]
[φαίνεται,] ξάνθᾳ δ᾽ ᾽Ελένᾳ σ᾽ ἐίσ[κ]ην
[ἔστιν ἔπει]κες

D 35, **E 44**, LP 23

112

῎Εστι μοι κάλα πάις χρυσίοισιν ἀνθέμοισιν
ἐμφέρην ἔχοισα μόρφαν, Κλεῖς ἀγαπάτα,
ἀντὶ τᾶς ἔγω οὐδὲ Λυδίαν παῖσαν οὐδ᾽ ἐράνναν
[Λέσβον ἀγρέην κε] . . .

D 152, **E 130**, LP 132

113

σοὶ δ᾽ ἔγω Κλέι ποικίλαν . . .
οὐκ ἔχω πόθεν ἔσσεται . . .
μιτράν[αν]· ἀλλὰ τὼι Μυτιληνάωι . . .

· · · · · · · · · ·

παιαειον ἔχην πο . . .
αἰκε η ποικιλασκ – – – – . . .

ταῦτα τὰς Κλεανακτιδα . . .
φύγας – – – ισαπολισεχει . . .
μνάμαι᾽· ἴδε γὰρ αἶνα διέρρυε[ν] . . .

D Suppl. pp. 39, 70, **LP 98b**

TO A FRIEND

When I look at you, it is not
Hermione I think of: a mortal girl,
but I am moved as before the beauty
of blond Helen.

KLEIS

I have a small daughter who is beautiful
like a gold flower. I would not trade
my darling Kleïs for all Lydia or even
for lovely Lesbos.

FROM HER EXILE

I have no embroidered headband
for you, Kleïs, and no idea
where to find one while Myrsilos

rules in Mytilene. The bright
ribbon reminds me of those days
when our enemies were in exile.

114

. . . [οὐδὲ θέ]μις σε Μίκα
. . . ελα[− − ἀλ]λά σ' ἔγωὐκ ἐάσω
. . . ν φιλότ[ατ'] ἤλεο Πενθιλήαν
. . . δα κα[κό]τροπ', ἄμμα . . .
. . . μέλ[ος] τι γλύκερον.
. . . α μελλιχόφων[ος] . . .
. . . [ἀεί]δει, λίγυραι δ' ἄη[δοι]
. . . δροσ[ό]εσσα . . .

D 70, LP 71

115

[Κύπρι κα]ὶ Νηρήιδες ἀβλάβη[ν μοι]
　[τὸν κασί]γνητον δ[ό]τε τυίδ' ἴκεσθα[ι]
　[κὤσσα F]οι θύμωι κε θέληι γένεσθαι
　　[πάντα τε] λέσθην,

[ὄσσα δὲ πρ]όσθ' ἄμβροτε πάντα λῦσα[ι]
　[καὶ φίλοις]ι Fοῖσι χάραν γένεσθαι
　　κὤνιαν [ἔ]χθροισι, γένοιτο δ' ἄμμι
　　. . . [μ]ηδ' εἶς·

[τὰν κασιγ]νήταν δὲ θέλοι πόησθαι
　. . .] οτοισι π[ά]ροιθ' ἀχεύων
　. . .] να

D 25, E 36, LP 5, P 5

BETRAYAL

You have done wrong, Mika,
and I will not concur:
you have chosen to be friends
with the house of Penthilos.
Yet now we hear a sweet intrusion,
a voice like honey
from the loud-singing nightingale
in the dewy branches.

TO APHRODITE AND THE NEREIDS

Kyprian and Nereids, I beg you
to bring my brother home safely,
and let him accomplish whatever
is in his heart.

Let him amend his former errors
and be a joy to his friends but
a terror to enemies — though never
again to us.

Let him do honor to his sister,
and be free of the black torment
which in other days of sorrow
ravaged his soul.

116

[Κύ]πρι κα[ί σ]ε πι[κροτ΄ – –]αν ἐπεύρ[οι]
[μη]δὲ καυχάσ[α]ιτο τόδ᾽ ἐννέ[ποισα]
[Δ]ωρίχα τὸ δεύ[τ]ερον ὡς πόθε[ννον]
[εἶς] ἔρον ἦλθε.

D 26, E 37, **LP 15**

117

  ... πων κάλα δῶρα παῖδες
  ... φίλ᾽, ἄοιδον λιγύραν χελύνναν

  ... [πά]ντα χρόα γῆρας ἤδη
[λεῦκαι τ᾽ ἐγένο]ντο τρίχες ἐκ μελαίναν

  ... αι· γόνα δ᾽ ο[ὐ] φέροισι
  ... ησθ᾽ ἴσα νεβρίοισιν

  ... [ἀ]λλὰ τί κεν ποείην;
  ... οὐ δύνατον γένεσθαι

    ... βροδόπαχυν Αὔων
  ... [ἔσ]χατα γᾶς φέροισα

  ... [Τίθω]νον ὔμως ἔμαρψε[ν]
  ... [ἐρ]άταν ἄκοιτιν

  ... [φθ]ιμέναν νομίσδει
  ... αις ὀπάσδοι

ἔγω δὲ φίλημμ᾽ ἀβροσύναν [– – –]τοῦτο καί μοι
τὸ λά[μπρον ἔρος τὠελίω καὶ τὸ κά[λ]λον λέ[λ]ογκε.

D 65a, E 118, LP 58

AGAINST DORICHA, HER BROTHER'S MISTRESS

Kyprian, may she find you harsh
and find no occasion to brag: I
Doricha, got my love to come back
    a second time.

AGE AND LIGHT

Here are fine gifts, children.
O friend, singer on the clear tortoise lyre,

all my flesh is wrinkled with age,
my black hair has faded to white,

my legs can no longer carry me,
once nimble like a fawn's,

but what can I do?
It cannot be undone,

no more than can pink-armed Dawn
not end in darkness on earth,

or keep her love for Tithonos,
who must waste away;

yet I love refinement, and beauty and light
are for me the same as desire for the sun.

118

"Ονοιϱε μελαινα . . .
φ[ο]ίταις ὄτα τ᾽ ὕπνος . . .

γλύκυς ϑ[έ]ος, ἦ δεῖν᾽ ὀνίας μ . . .
ζὰ χῶϱις ἔχην τὰν δυναμ[ιν] . . .

ἔλπις δέ μ᾽ ἔχει μὴ πεδέχη[ν] . . .
μηδὲν μακάϱων ἐλ . . .

οὐ γάϱ κ᾽ ἔον οὔτω . . .
ἀϑύϱματα κα . . .

γένοιτο δέ μοι . . .
τοὶς πάντα . . .

D 67, E 118 B (App.), LP 63

DREAM

O dream from the blackness,
come when I am sleeping.

Sweet is the god but still I am
in agony and far from my strength,

for I had no hope to share
something of the happy ones,

nor was I so foolish
as to scorn pleasant toys.

Now may I have
all these things.

119

ἐπιάξατε . . .
δάφνας ὄτα . . .

πὰν δ᾽ ἄδιον . . .
ἢ κῆνον ἐλὸ . . .

καὶ ταῖσι μὲν ἀ . . .
ὀδοίπορος ἂν . . .

μόγις δέ ποτ᾽ εἰσάιον· ἐκλ . . .
ψύχα δ᾽ αγαπάτα συν . . .

τέαντ[–] δὲ νῦν ἔμμ[ατα] . . .
ἴκεσθ᾽ ἀγανα . . .

ἔφθατε· κάλαν . . .
τά τ᾽ ἔμματα κα[ὶ] . . .

D 66, E 118 A (App.), LP 62

THE LAUREL TREE

You lay in wait
behind a laurel tree,

and everything
was pleasant:

you a woman
wanderer like me.

I barely heard you,
my darling;

you came in your
trim garments,

and suddenly: beauty
of your garments.

120

Τῷ γρίππει Πελάγωνι πάτηρ ἐπέθηκε Μένισκος
κύρτον καὶ κώπαν, μνᾶμα κακοζοίας.

D 159, **E 145**

121

'Ασαροτέρας οὐδαμά ποι Εἴρηνα σέθεν τύχοισα

D 64, **E 116**, LP 91

122

[Μακραι]ονίαν τε κὐγίειαν
[Τὰ βρύσ]σα φύγοιμι, παῖδες· ἤβα ...

E 113 A, B, LP Incert. 18

FOR PELAGON

Pelagon the fisherman. His father
Meniskos placed here a fishbasket
and oar: relics of a wretched life.

EMPTINESS

I have never found you
so repulsive, O peace.

A WOMAN'S PLEA

I pray for long life and health.
My children, I would escape
from wrinkles and cling to youth.

123

Σαπφὼ (φησιν) ὅτι
τὸ ἀποθνήσκειν κακόν· οἱ θεοὶ γὰρ οὕτω κεκρίκασιν·
ἀπέθνησκον γὰρ ἄν.

E 91, **LP 201**

124

Τίμαδος ἅδε κόνις, τὰν δὴ πρὸ γάμοιο θάνοισαν
δέξατο Φερσεφόνας κυάνιος θάλαμος,
ἇς καὶ ἀπυφθιμένας παῖσαι νεόθαγι σιδάρῳ
ἄλικες ἱμμέρταν κρᾶτος ἔθεντο κόμαν.

D 158, **E 144**

125

[κ]αδδέκεται μέλαινα
πόλλων ἀχέων ἐπαύσθη
Ἀτρεΐδαι τελέσθη[ν] . . .

LP Incert. 27, **T p. 16**

SAPPHO SAYS:

Death is our evil. The gods believe this,
  or else by now they would be dead.

ON TIMAS

Here is the dust of Timas who unmarried
was led into Persephone's dark bedroom,
and when she died her girlfriends took sharp
iron knives and cut off their soft hair.

ACHILLES

He lies now in the black earth,
and the many sorrows are ended
which he bore for the Atreides.

126

[Φοίβωι χρυσοκό]μαι τὸν ἔτικτε Κόω [κόρα]
[μίγεισ᾽ εὐρυβίαι Κρ]ονίδαι μεγαλωνύμω[ι]
[Ἄρτεμις δὲ θέων] μέγαν ὅρκον ἐπώμοσε
[– – – κεφά]λαν· ἀιπάρθενος ἔσσομαι
[κοἰκήσω μεγά]λων ὀρέων κορύφαισ᾽ ἔπι
[θηρεύοισα· σὺ καὶ τό]δε νεῦσον ἔμαν χάριν.
[τᾶι δὲ πάντ᾽ ἐπένευ]σε θέων μακάρων πάτηρ.
[– – – ἐλαφάβο]λον ἀγροτέραν μέγα·
[οὐδ᾽ αὔται γάμος οὔτ᾽ ἔρος οὐδάμα πίλαται.

D 102, E 152, LP Alc. 304, T p. 7

127

φαῖσι δή ποτα Λήδαν ὑακίνθινον
πεπυκάδμενον ὤιον
εὔρην

D 105, E 97, LP 166

ARTEMIS

To blond Apollo — child of Koios' daughter
after she lay with our famous lord Zeus —
Artemis swore an oath of the gods,
swore by the beard of her father:
"I shall always be a virgin
and live on summits of the great sierras,
hunting in the forests: O grant me this!"
Her father nodded in approval. Now gods
and mortals call her by her thrilling name:
the deer-slaying hunter,
and she is pure of marriage or erotic love.

THE SWAN'S GIFT

It is said that Leda long ago
found a hidden egg the color
of hyacinths.

128

ἀλλ' ἔων φίλος ἄμμι
λέχος ἄρνυσο νεώτερον·
οὐ γὰρ τλάσομ' ἔγω συνοί-
κην ἔοισα γεραιτέρα . . .

D 100, E 99, **LP 121**

129

ἀλγεσίδωρος

μυθόπλοκος

E 28, **LP 172, 188**

130

ἔμεθεν δ' ἔχηισθα λάθαν

D 146, E 124, **LP 129, l. 1**

IT IS LATE

Even if you love me, find
a younger woman. I could
never bear to share my bed
with a man younger than I.

BITTERSWEET LOVE

It brings us pain
and weaves myths.

YOU FORGOT

And I am now wholly
gone into oblivion.

131

ταὶς κάλαισιν ὔμμι νόημμα τὦμον
οὐ διάμειπτον

D 12, E 14, **LP 41**

132

Ἔσπερε πάντα φέρων ὅσα φαίνολις ἐσκέδασ᾿ Αὔως,
φέρεις ὄιν, φέρεις αἶγα, φέρεις ἄπυ μάτερι παῖδα.

D 120, E 149, **LP 104a**

133

[Ἔρ-]
μας γ᾿ εἴσηλθ᾿ ἐπ᾿ ὀ[νοίρατός μ᾿· ἔγω δὲ]
εἶπον· ῏Ω δέσποτ᾿ ἔπ[παν ὀλώλαμεν·]
οὐ μὰ γὰρ μάκαιραν [ἔγωγ᾿]
οὐδὲν ἄδομ᾿ ἔπαρθ᾿ ἄγα[ν ἔτ᾿ ὄλβῳ,]
καιθάνην δ᾿ ἴμερός τις [ἔχει με καὶ]
λωτίνοις δροσόεντας [ὄχ-]
θοις ἴδην Ἀχέρ[οντος] . . .

D 97, **E 85**, LP 95

HER FRIENDS

No, my heart can never change
toward you who are so lovely.

EVENING STAR

Hesperos, you bring home all the bright dawn
        disperses,
bring home the sheep,
bring home the goat, bring the child home to its
        mother.

TO HERMES

Hermes came to me in a dream. I said
— My master, I am altogether lost,
and my many riches do not console me.
I care only
                to die, and watch the dewy lotus
along the banks of Acheron, river of Hell.

134

[αἰ δέ μοι γάλακτο]ς ἐπάβολ᾽ ἦσ[κε]
[τωῦθατ᾽ ἢ παίδ]ων δόλοφυν [ποήσ]ει
[ἀρμένα, τάχ᾽ οὐ] τρομέροις πρ[ὸς] ἄλλα
[λέκτρα κε πόσσι]

[ἠρχόμαν· νῦν δὲ] χρόα γῆρας ἤδη
[μυρίαν ἄμμον ῥύτι]ν ἀμφιβάσκει,
[κωὖ πρὸς ἄμμ᾽ Ἔρο]ς πέταται διώκων
[ἀλγεσίδωρος.]

. . . τᾶς ἀγαύας
. . . έα· λάβοισα
. . . ἄεισον ἄμμι
τὰν ἰόκολπον

D 32, **E 42**, LP 21

135

οὐ γὰρ θέμις ἐν μοισοπόλων οἰκίαι
θρῆνον ἔμμεν᾽· οὔ κ᾽ ἄμμι τάδε πρέποι

D 109, E 108, **LP 150**

LAST PRAISES

If my nipples were to drip milk
and my womb still carry a child,
I would enter this marriage bed
        intrepidly,

but age dries my flesh with a thousand
wrinkles, and love is in no hurry
to seize my body with the gifts
        of pleasant pain.

Yet, let us sing praises to her
who wears the scent of violets
        on her young breasts.

TO HER DAUGHTER
WHEN SAPPHO WAS DYING

It would be wrong for us. It is not right
for mourning to enter a home of poetry.

136

ἀλλ' ἔμ' ὀλβίαν ἀδόλως ἔθηκαν
χρύσιαι Μοῖσαι οὐδ' ἔμεθεν θανοίσας
ἔσσεται λάθα

E 11, LP 193

137

μνάσεσθαί τινά φαιμ' ἄψερον ἀμμέων

λάθα μέν τινας ἐψεύσαιο κἀτέροις
ἀ δ' ἄνδρων ἀγάθων οὐδενα πώποτα
γνώμα . . .

D 59, E 76, 77, LP 147

138

[Αΐδας θεῶν]
μόνος οὐ δέκεται γλυκερᾶς μέρος ἐλπίδος

D Monodia, 18, E Lyra graeca, III, p. 438

HER WEALTH

The golden Muses gave me
true riches: when dead
I shall not be forgotten.

SOMEONE, I TELL YOU

Someone, I tell you,
will remember us.

We are oppressed by
fears of oblivion

yet are always saved
by judgment of good men.

HADES

In all the dominions of the gods
only Death allows no place for sweet hope.

139

]θε θῦμον
]μι πάμπαν
]δύναμαι,
]
]ας κεν ἦι μοι
]σαντιλάμπην
]λον πρόσωπον.
]
]γχροῖσθεις,
       ]΄[..]ρος

D 24, E 34, **LP 4**

EROS

Now in my
heart I
see clearly

a beautiful
face
shining,

etched
by love.

140

πυφα[

Ανδ]ρομε[δ-
   ]δελασ[

   ]ροτήννεμε[
Ψάπφοι, σὲ φίλ[ημμ'

Κύπρωι βασίληα[
καί τοι μέγα δ.[

[ὄ]σσοις φαέθων ἀ[έλιος
πάνται κλέος[

καί σ' ἐνν ᾽Αχέρ[οντος
[.]ρ[. . . . .] νπ[

D 68, LP 65

SAPPHO, I LOVED YOU

Andromeda
forgot,

and I too
blamed you,

yet Sappho
I loved you.

In Kypros I am Queen
and to you a power

as sun of fire
is a glory to all.

Even in Hades
I am with you.

ADDENDA

Other Words and Phrases
Attributed to Sappho

141

ἤ σε Κύπρος καὶ Πάφος ἢ Πάνορμος

D 7, E 5, LP 35

142

].αν, ἔγω δ᾽ ἔμ᾽ αὔται
]τοῦτο συ]νοίδα

D 37, E 15, LP 26, (ll. 11-12)

143

κὰτ ἔμον στάλαχμον

D 14, E 17, LP 37

144

φαίνεταί Ϝοι κῆνος

D 3, E 26, LP 165

141

Whether at Kypros and Paphos or at Panormos.
(Of Aphrodite).

142

All this I see plainly now.

143

Because of my pain.

144

That (man) seems to himself.

145

τ᾽ ἐξ ἀδοκή[τ

D 27b, E 39, **LP 16 (l. 12)**

146

οὔ τί μοι ὔμμες

D 43, E 49

147

ᾶς θέλει᾽ ὔμμες

D 44, E 50, **LP 45**

148

στεφάνοισι σελιννίνοις

E 64, LP 191

145

Unexpectedly.

146

You are nothing to me.

147

As long as you wish.

148

Garlands of celery.

149

τὸν Ϝὸν παῖδα κάλει

D 112, E 79, **LP 164**

150

Γέλλως παιδοφιλωτέρα

D 104, E 95, **LP 178**

151

αὔτα δὲ σὺ Καλλιόπα

D 155, E 127, **LP 124**

152

τίοισιν ὀφθάλμοισι(ν);

D 156a, E 132, **LP 162**

149

He whom she calls her son.

150

(She) loves children even more than Gello does.

151

You yourself Kalliope.

152

With what eyes? (i.e., How will you dare look at me?)

153

αἰμιτύβιον στάλασσον

D 153, E 131, **LP 119**

154

δώσομεν, ἦσι πάτηρ

D 122, E 153, **LP 109**

155

πότνια Αὔως

D 16, E 177, **LP 157**

153

A dripping dishcloth.

154

"We shall give," said the father.

155

The queenly dawn.

156

χρυσαστράγαλοι φίαλαι

D 133a, E 191, **LP 192**

157

ὦ τὸν Ἄδωνιν

D 21, E 25, **LP 168**

158

τεσσεραμήνιον
ὦ τὸν Ἀδώνιον

D 132b, **E 136**, LP Incert. 24

156

Gold cup with a knuckle-like base.

157

Poor Adonis!

158

Poor Adonis of the four-month sojourns.

There are also single words quoted by the ancient commentators. English and Greek words follow:

myrrh μύρραν, E 63

little Timas Τιμαδία, E 88

guileless or ingenuous ἄκακος, LP 171

dawn αὔα, LP 175

water trench ἀμάρα, LP 174

vines on trees ἀμαμάξυδ(-ος, -ες), LP 173

coffer γρύτα, LP 179

a fordable stream ζάβατον, LP 181

I might lead ἀγαγοίην, LP 169

soda or nitron νίτρον, LP 189

very learned πολυίδριδι, LP 190

Scythian wood Σκύθικον ξύλον, LP 210

Medea Μήδεϊα, LP 186

of the Muses Μοισάων, LP 187

Aiga — a promontory of Kanaia Αἶγα, LP 170

danger κίνδυν, LP 184

shift βεῦδος, LP 177

Hektor Ἕκτωρ, LP 180

barbitos, baromos, barmos (ancient instruments) βάρβιτος. βάρωμος. βάρμος. LP 176

A number of fragments, usually in columns and sometimes mere syllables or single letters, are so mutilated that they have little or no meaning. They are mainly of paleographical interest, though their separate words may give clues to subject matter, and with much irreverent daring some may one day be restored, as Lobel, Bowra, Edmonds, and Treu have done on occasion. These fragments are: Lobel-Page 6-14, 18, 19, 24b-c, 25, 28, 29, 59, 60, 61, 64, 66-70, 72-81, 82b, 83-88, 90, 93, 97, 99, 103, 139, 161, 213; i.a.2,26,27; attributed to Sappho by Treu but to Alkaios by Page are: Lobel-Page 255, 256, 257, Schol. Alk 259, 261 col. I, II, 263, 304, col. II. In Diehl but omitted by Page is Diehl 72. New fragments are: (fr. novum) P. Ox 2357 fr. 1, (fr. novum) P. Ox. 2357 fr. 4.

GLOSSARY AND INDEX

Acheron. The river of Death running through Hades. It began in Thesprotia, Epiros, and disappeared underground in places where it was supposed to lead to Hades. 133

Achilles. Son of Peleus and the sea nymph (the Nereid) Thetis. He is the tragic hero of Homer's *Iliad*. 125

Adonis. Aphrodite's beautiful young lover. He was killed by a wild boar or by Ares or Hephaistos but was allowed to spend six months of each year upon the earth with Aphrodite, the remainder with Persephone in the underworld. Thus he was identified with the seeding and harvesting of crops and was worshiped, especially by women, as divinity of vegetation and fertility. In Sappho 158 Adonis spends four months with Aphrodite, four months with Persephone, and four months alone. 35, 69, 157, 158

Alkaios (Alcaeus). Born about 620 B.C. in Mytilene, Lesbos. A poet, contemporary and possible friend or lover of Sappho, he wrote lyric poems that deal with politics, love, drinking, the sea, in the Aiolic (Lesbian) dialect. The Alcaic strophe was imitated by Horace. 82

Amorgine. Of Amorgos, an island of the Aigaion Sea, one of the Sporades, known for its Amorgine linen. It was the birthplace of Semonides. 90

Anaktoria. One of Sappho's friends. One theory is that she left Sappho in order to marry and follow her husband to Sardis, where he was probably a soldier. 5, 22

Andromache. The wife of Hektor, the Trojan hero. 68

Andromeda. A rival of Sappho; perhaps a poet. 25, 71, 72, 73, 140

Aphrodite. Goddess of love, beauty, sea, flowers, and fertility. She was born in the seafoam (*aphros*) off the shore of Paphos in Kypros (Cyprus) and so is called variously Kypris (Cypris), Kyprian (Cyprian), Kypros-born (Cyprus-born), and the Paphian (of Paphos). As a symbol of passion and romantic love, she is a particular ally to Sappho and is mentioned by Sappho in the existing fragments more often than any other deity or person. The one complete poem attributed to Sappho, 28, is addressed to Aphrodite. 28, 29, 33, 36, 38, 39, 40, 41, 47, 57, 65, 69, 115

Apollo. Apollo and his twin sister Artemis were born in Delos, children of Zeus and Leto. God of prophecy, music, medicine; as sun-god identified with Helios. He was the ideal of young, manly beauty and of civilized Greek man. 68, 126

Ares. Greek war-god and personification of warrior type. In Rome he was the more popular Mars. 58, 76

Artemis. Twin sister of Apollo (q.v.), she was the virgin goddess of the forest and hunting and of the moon. 126

Atreidai. Sons or descendants of Atreus, usually referring to Agamemnon and Menelaos. 30, 125

Atthis. One of Sappho's friends, treated with deep affection in many poems. Like Anaktoria (q.v.), she leaves Sappho. 21, 22, 23, 24, 25, 26

Chian. Of the island of Chios, a large island south of Lesbos, near Asia Minor. 23

Cretan, Crete. Large island in the Aigaion with capital of Minoan civilization at Knossos. 29, 64

Dika. Probably short for Mnasidika (q.v.), one of Sappho's friends. 95

Dionysos. God of vegetation, wine, and spiritual ecstasy, he was worshiped with orgiastic rites and often represents the counterpart of Apollonian moderation. Also called Bakchos (Bacchus). 30

Eros. God of love, child or attendant of Aphrodite. Sappho makes Eros the son of Gaia (Earth) and Ouranos (Sky) but she most often uses Eros to mean simply love; these many references are not cited here. 7, 33, 34

Atlas and Eos (Dawn), and father of the Hesperides. 19, 132

Hymen, Hymenaios. God of marriage, a handsome youth whom it was customary to invoke at Greek weddings by singing Hymen, O Hymen, in the hymneal or bridal song. 58

Ida. The herald or messenger who is probably from Ida, a mountain area near Troy. In the *Iliad*, 3. 248-258, he appears as the chief herald of Troy. 68

Ilios (Ilus). Son of Tros and founder of Ilium (Troy). Ilium was the city of Ilios but was also called Troy after his father, Tros. Homer's *Iliad* deals with the siege of Ilium (Troy). 68

Ilium (Troy). City of Ilios (q.v.). 68

Ionian. Greeks in an area of the west coast of Asia Minor. 24

Jason. Leader of the Argonauts who set sail in the Argo to find the Golden Fleece, which he hoped to bring his uncle Pelias in exchange for his patrimony. He obtained the fleece with the help of Medea, whom he later married. 91

Kalliope. Muse of heroic poetry (See Muses).

Kleïs. Name of Sappho's daughter, also her mother, and perhaps a friend. 23, 112, 113

Knossos. Ancient capital of the Minoan kingdom and site of the palace of Minos, which has been associated with the labyrinth and the minotaur (the bull of Minos). 29

Koios. A Titan, mother of Leto and hence grandmother of Apollo and Artemis. 126

Kyprian (Cyprian) or Kypris (Cypris). One from Kypros (Cyprus), in this case Aphrodite (q.v.). 31, 84, 115, 116

Kypros (Cyprus), Kypros-born (Cyprus-born). The large Greek island of Kypros (Cyprus), near the coast of Syria, was one of the chief seats of worship of Aphrodite. The Kypros-born (Cyprus-born) is Aphrodite (q.v.). 32, 37, 68, 140, 141

Kythereia. Of the island of Kythera, southeast of Lakonia, Peloponnesos, a seat of worship of Aphrodite. Hence the goddess was called Kythereia. There was also a tradition that Aphrodite rose from the sea near Kythera (See Aphrodite). 35

Leda. Mother of Helen, the Dioskouroi, and in some versions Klytemnestra, and wife of Tyndareus. She was seduced by Zeus, who came to her, as readers of Yeats know, in the form of a swan. Another version, to which Sappho alludes, has Nemesis lay an egg which Leda found and cared for and from which came Helen. 127

Meniskos. Father of Pelagon. 120

Mika. Probably a shortened form of Mnasidika (q.v.), a rival who had gone over to the rival house of Penthilos, ruling nobles of Mytilene. 114

Mnasidika. A friend of Sappho's who appears to have deserted her (See Mika). 96

Muses. Daughters of Zeus and Mnemosyne (Memory), the nine Muses lived on Mount Helikon, where they presided over the arts and sciences. 43, 44, 45, 136

Myrsilos. Tyrant of Mytilene who probably caused the exile of Alkaios and Sappho. 113

Mytilene, Mitylene. Ancient and modern capital of Lesbos, where Sappho spent much of her life. The dialect of Lesbos was Aiolic, in which Sappho and Alkaios wrote. 23, 100, 113

Nereids. Sea Nymphs, fifty daughters of Nereus, the old man of the sea. 115

Nereus. Son of Pontos, husband of the Oceanid Doris, and father of the Nereids, Nereus was the wise old man of the sea. 86

Niobe. Daughter of Tantalos and wife of Amphion, Niobe boasted to Leto that her family was larger than Leto's, and to avenge this insult Leto's children, Apollo and Artemis, killed the twelve to twenty children of Niobe. Niobe became a stock figure of bereavement (see *Testimonia*). 77

Pandion. King of Athens whose daughters Philomela and Prokne were turned into a swallow and a nightingale. (Latin tradition reversed the order.) The presence of a swallow was often the sign of a forthcoming event. 78

Panormos. One of several Greek cities with this name

where Aphrodite was worshiped, but not the most famous Panormos (Palermo) in Sicily. Palermo did not acquire its Greek name until after Sappho's time. 141

Paphian. Of Paphos, and therefore Aphrodite. Aphrodite was born in the foam near the city of Paphos in Kypros (Cyprus) (see Aphrodite). 55

Paphos. (See Paphian and Aphrodite.) 141

Peitho. The personification of Persuasion, and the daughter or attendant of Aphrodite. 41, 69

Pelagon. A fisherman. 120

Penthilos. A rival family of ruling nobles in Mytilene (see Mika, Mnasidika). Pittakos, Tyrant of Lesbos in Sappho's time, married the sister of Drakon, former ruler, who was the son of Penthilos. 114

Persephone. Closely associated with her mother, Demeter, Persephone was abducted by Hades and taken to the underworld. Her yearly return to earth signified the coming of spring. 124

Pierian. Of Pieria, a region of Thrace in Macedonia, where the Muses were first worshiped. 80

Phokaia. A city of Ionia in Asia Minor, southeast of Mytilene. 36

Plakia. A river near Thebes (q.v.) in the area near Troy. 68

Pleiades. Daughters of Atlas and virgin companions of Artemis. When pursued by the giant hunter Orion, their prayers were answered when they were changed into doves (*peleiades*) and placed among the stars. 6

Praxinoa. One of Sappho's companions. 23

Priam. King of Troy at time of the Achaian attack, father of Hektor (q.v.). 68

Psappho. In her own Aiolic dialect, Sappho referred to herself as Psappho (see Sappho).

Sappho. Born about 612 B.C. in Eresos or Mytilene, Lesbos, Sappho wrote lyric poems in her own Aiolic dialect in which she referred to herself as Psappho. 28, 33, 47, 82, 123, 140

Sardis. Ancient city of Asia Minor and capital of the kingdom of Lydia. 3, 22

Thebe, Thebes. Not the more famous cities of Boioteia or

SOURCES AND NOTES

For more information about the poems, see *Glossary*, or *Testimonia* when indicated. Many lines of Sappho have been saved in the ancient commentaries: those remarks which immediately precede or follow Sappho's lines are given below except where they are purely linguistic in nature. The poem number, in brackets, precedes each entry.

[1] Hermogenes, *On Kinds of Oratory*, 3.317 Walz. The grammarian Orion in *Etymologicum*, 28.15, also cites the word χέλυννα, tortoise or lyre, and the word is probably from this same fragment cited by Hermogenes.

[2] From a vase painting of the middle of the fifth century B.C. *Museo Italiano* ii, pl. 6. This introductory poem may have stood at the beginning of Sappho's poems. Haines reads ἀνα[ι]τίων where Edmonds reads ὀνάτων.

[3] From a third-century papyrus, in Copenhagen, first published by Vogliano in a booklet entitled *Sappho: una nuova della poetessa* (Milan, 1941). In this intimate domestic poem addressed to her daughter Kleïs, Sappho contrasts an artificial adornment with the natural, inexpensive adornment of a wreath of fresh flowers, which is, in any case, more appropriate for one with fair hair. Another reference to Kleïs' blond hair is suggested in 112. Another reason for a natural adornment, however, is implied in the fragment that follows in Greek, 113, where Sappho seems to speak of poverty, possibly during exile, when an elaborate headband was probably more than she could afford.

[4] *Etymologicum Magnum*, 2.43. This may be addressed to one of her rivals, to Gorgo or to Andromeda.

[5] From a second-century papyrus, *Oxyrhynchus Papyri*, 1231.1. i (B). The last four fragmentary lines, 21–24, which Edmonds restores largely by conjecture, are omitted. Sappho begins the poem with a paratactic trope, found also in Tyrtaios, fr.9 D, and Pindar, Olympian I, to compare the apparent splendor of military spectacles with the power of love. While she does not dull the public sparkle of the masculine world of war, to her all this bright clutter of history cannot match the illumination of love and physical beauty in her personal world. See *Glossary* for Anaktoria.

[6] Hephaistion, *Handbook of Meter*, 70. Although this is one of the two or three best-known poems attributed to Sappho, her authorship is now denied by recent editors. The poem is Lesbian, however, and a simple yet impeccable example of her imagery and ideas.

[7] Apollonios, *On Pronouns*, 100.5.

[8] Maximus of Tyre, *Dissertations*, 24.9.

[9] Longinus, *On the Sublime*, 10. I have followed Edmonds' text, except for βρόχε᾽ line 7, which I have read not as a name, *Brocheo*, but as βρόχε᾽, *for a moment* or *now*. Catullus' fifty-first ode to Lesbia — Lesbia for the Lesbian Sappho — is an imitation of Sappho's poem:

> Ille mi par esse deo videtur,
> ille, si fas est, superare divos,
> qui sedens adversus identidem te
>   spectat et audit
>
> dulce ridentem, misero quod omnis
> eripit sensus mihi: nam simul te,
> Lesbia, aspexi, nihil est super mi
>   . . .
>
> lingua sed torpet, tenuis sub artus
> flamma demanat, sonitu suopte
> tintinant aures, gemina teguntur
>   lumina nocte.

For the context in which Sappho's poem appears see Longinus, *The Sublime*, in Testimonia section.

A recent tradition of scholarship holds this poem to be

a wedding song to be sung before a bride and groom. There is no internal evidence of this, and were this to be true, these verses of violent personal passion would be inappropriate at the ceremony. The poem is a marvel of candor and power in which Sappho states her jealousy of the calm godlike man and describes with striking objectivity and detachment the physical symptoms of her passionate love for the girl.

Some years before, Archilochos, the first poet to speak of passions of the outsider and individual, had written:

> I lie here miserable and broken with desire,
> pierced through to the bones by the bitterness
> of this god-given painful love.
>
> O comrade, this passion makes my limbs limp
> and tramples over me. fr. 104 D.

[10] Herodianos, *Words without Parallel*, 2.912.10 Lentz. Horace wrote: "Sublimi feriam sidera vertice." (*Carmina*, I, i, 36)

[11] Athenaios, *Doctors at Dinner*, 2.54 f.

[12] Scholiast on Apollonios of Rhodes, *Argonautika*, 1.1123.

[13] Athenaios, *Doctors at Dinner*, 13.571 d, writes: "Free women and girls call a friend or acquaintance *hetaira* as Sappho does: [poem follows]." The verse shows that hetaira, as used by Sappho, signified *comrade*, not *courtesan*.

[14] Eustathios on the *Iliad*, 729.20. The word *silver*, ἀργυρία, first suggested by Blomfield appears in Edmonds; Bowra suggests it, but it does not appear in Diehl and Page.

[15] Ammonios, *Words that Differ*, 23. The word *thief* is not in the Greek text.

[16] Demetrios, *On Style*, 142. This fragment is also attributed to Alkaios (E. 161). Alkaios' poem begins:

> Wash your gullet with wine for the dog-star returns
> with the heat of summer searing a thirsting earth.
> Cicadas cry softly under high leaves, and pour down
> shrill song incessantly from under their wings. (Fr. 94 D)

Alkaios' poem is itself a version of lines by Hesiod in *Works and Days*.

[17] Scholiast on Pindar, *Pythian* 1.10, writes: He [Pindar] has described a picture of an eagle perched on Zeus' scepter and lulled to sleep by music, letting both wings lie still. . . . On the other hand Sappho says of pigeons: [poem follows]."

[18] Scholiast on Sophokles, El. 149, writes: "The phrase messenger or herald of Zeus is used of the nightingale because it is a sign of the coming of spring. Sappho writes: [poem follows]." Ben Jonson took from this fragment his line in *The Sad Shepherd*, Act II: "The dear good angel of the Spring, The Nightingale." He gave Sappho's word ἄγγελος, herald, or messenger, its later Biblical meaning of *angel*.

[19] Himerios, *Declamations*, 13.9. Himerius cites this fragment from an "Ode to Hesperos" by Sappho.

[20] Demetrios, *On Style*, 164, writes: "Charm and also elegant effects occur when the most beautiful words are used as in: [poem follows]"

[21] Pollux, *Vocabulary*, 10.124.

[22] From a seventh-century manuscript, *Berliner Klassikertexte*, p. 9722.5. The first line is Edmonds' conjecture and the only certain word of the second line is Sardis; yet the line is appropriate, as a title if nothing else, in order to show the probable relationship between Atthis and her friend who has gone off to distant Sardis (see poem 5). Her friend may be Anaktoria, or, as other commentators have suggested, Gongyla or Arignota, or someone else.

[23] From a seventh-century manuscript, *Berliner Klassikertexte*, p. 9722.1. The first line "In your own words, Atthis, you said" is added in order to indicate the speaker. Sappho's name appears here as Psappho, in her native Aiolic. The Greek for *breakfast* is literally *sweet drink*.

[24] From the reverse side of *ms* in 22, *Berliner Klassikertexte*, p. 9722.2. The first line and several of the last are in large part restored by Edmonds.

[25] Hephaistion, *Handbook of Meter*, 46 (see *Testimonia*).

[26] Terentianus Maurus, *On Meters*, 6.390 Keil, writes: "[Sappho] . . . sings that Atthis was small in those days when her own girlhood was blossoming."

[27] From a second-century papyrus, *Oxyrhynchus Papyri*, 1231.13, extensively restored by Edmonds. The poem recalls the spirit and language of Kavafis' modern Greek poem "*Ὁ Θεὸς ἀπολείπει Ἀντώνιον* [The god Forsakes Anthony]."

[28] Dionysios of Halikarnassos, *Literary Composition*, 23. The Page text is used, as it appears in *Sappho and Alcaeus*, Denys Page, Oxford, 1955. Page has not included the brackets in this edition. He does use brackets in the Lobel-Page text of the same poem, but his brackets do not mean a conjectural supplement, as they do in Edmonds' texts, but merely doubt or obvious restoration. This poem to Aphrodite is usually considered the one complete poem that has survived of Sappho. There are fragments of other poems, however, which have more lines than this complete poem. Despite the tone of intimate friendship and even gay camaraderie, the poem has the formal structure of a prayer with the expected invocation, sanction, and entreaty.

[29] From the third century B.C. ostracon, ed. by Norsa, *Annali della reale Scuola normale superiore di Pisa, Lettere, Storia e Filosofia*, Serie ii. vol. vi. 1937. The text is from Bowra's *Greek Lyric Poetry* but I reproduced Diehl's reading of line 10, substituting Diehl's *πρωινίοισιν* for Bowra and Page's *ἠρίνοισιν*. Crete was thought to be the original seat of worship of Aphrodite, or so its inhabitants claimed. While the scene described appears real and particular, the elements are relevant to the worship of Aphrodite. Apples and horses were symbols of Aphrodite, who was known as Aphrodite of the apples as well as Aphrodite of the horses. The prayer for epiphany in the poem is by no means proof that Sappho was a priestess or a poet of cult songs. Her concern with Aphrodite was with a figure that represented beauty and love.

[30] From a second-century and a third-century papyrus, *Oxyrhynchus Papyri*, 1231.1. ii (B). The text is from Page's *Sappho and Alcaeus*. Page makes helpful supplements and

restorations. Sappho's poem suggests that the Atreidai, Agamemnon and Menelaos, left Troy together and reached Lesbos together. This Lesbian version differs from Homer's (*Odyssey* III) in which Menelaos leaves Agamemnon at Troy and reaches Lesbos alone.

[31] Hephaistion, *Handbook of Meter*, 65.

[32] Aristotle, *Nikomachean Ethics*, 1149b.15, writes: "For desire is cunning, as is said about Aphrodite: [poem follows]." The title and words "For I am" are added to indicate the speaker.

[33] Maximus of Tyre, *Dissertations*, 24 (18).9, writes: "Diotima [in Plato's *Symposium*] tells Sokrates that Eros is not the son but the attendant and servant of Aphrodite, and in a poem Aphrodite says to Sappho: [poem follows]."

[34] Scholiast on Apollonius of Rhodes, *Argonautika*, 3.26, writes: "Apollonios makes Eros the son of Aphrodite but Sappho makes him the child of Gaia [Earth] and Ouranos [sky]."

Scholiast on Theokritos, 13.2, writes: "He is uncertain of whom to make Eros the son. Hesiod . . . and Sappho make him the son of Gaia [Earth] and Ouranos [Sky]."

Pausanias, *Description of Greece*, 9, 27.2, writes: "It is written that Hesiod made Chaos the first creation, then Gaia [Earth] and Tartaros and Eros. And in the poems of Sappho the Lesbian there are many mutually inconsistent statements about Eros: [poem follows]." The text used here has been restored by Edmonds.

[35] Hephaistion, *Handbook of Meter*, 64 (see *Testimonia*).

[36] Athenaios, *Doctors at Dinner*, 9.410 e, writes: "When Sappho in her Fifth Book of Lyric Poems says to Aphrodite [poem follows] she means the handkerchief as an adornment for the head, as indicated also by Hekataios, or some other writer, in the book entitled *Guide to Asia* where he writes 'Women wear handkerchiefs on their heads.'" The reading is difficult. Edmonds inserts Timas, gratuitously; Diehl finds Mnasis in the poem; Page finds no distinct lady at all.

[37] Hephaistion, *Handbook of Meter*, 74.

[38] Apollonios, *Pronouns*, 81.23. Other readings of the

fragment interpret the first and last phrase as "I will bring
to the altar" and "I shall pour a libation for you."

[39] Apollonios, *Syntax*, 350(247).

[40] Philodemos, *Piety*, 42. Lobel-Page places these lines
in the *Incertum utrius auctoris fragmenta* section of the
poems of Sappho and Alkaios.

[41] Scholiast on Hesiod, *Works and Days*, 73, writes:
"Sappho calls Peitho [Persuasion] the daughter of Aphrodite." Edmonds restores the Greek line.

[42] *Argument to Theokritos*, 28.

[43] Hephaistion, *Handbook of Meter*, 101.

[44] Hephaistion, *Handbook of Meter*, 106.

[45] Apollonios, *Pronouns*, 113.8.

[46] *Etymologicum Magnum*, 250.10.

[47] Hephaistion, *Handbook of Meter*, 87. In place of
"Why do you condemn?" others read "Why honor?"

[48] Aldus, *Cornucopia*, 14.9 (see *Testimonia*).

[49] Scholiast on Hermogenes, *Kinds of Style*, 1.1,
writes: "Some kinds of style have to do with one kind of
thought only . . . others . . . express things pleasing to the
senses of sight, hearing, smell, taste, touch, such as Homer's *Iliad* 347 f or Sappho's: [Like a sweet apple, etc.]"
Demetrios, *On Style*, 106, writes: "The epiphonema, as it
is called, may be considered as a phrase that adds adornment, and elevates style . . . For example, the sense is in-
tensified by such a phrase as "like the hyacinth" . . . while
it is adorned by the succeeding words "and it still blooms."
Himerios, *Declamations*, 9–16, writes: "Sappho compared
a virgin to an apple, allowing those who would pluck it
before its time not even to touch it with their fingertips,
but he who would pick it in the right season might watch
its beauty grow; compared the bridegroom to Achilles and
his deeds to the hero's." In Theokritos, *Idyll*, 18.38, Catullus, 11.21-24, and Virgil, *Aeneid*, 9.435, also occur Sappho's words.

[50] Philostratos, *Pictures*, 2.1, and Aristainetos, *Letters*,
1.10, both refer to the phrase honey- or gentle-voiced as
Sappho's most delightful epithet, and on this basis Edmonds suggests the phrase "to gentle-voiced maidens."

[51] Scholiast on Aristophanes, *Thesm.* 401 writes: "Gar-

lands were woven by young people and lovers. This refers
to the custom where among the people of antiquity the
women wove garlands: [poem follows]."

[52] Hephaistion, *Handbook on Dactylics*, 44.

[53] From a second-century papyrus, *Oxyrhynchus Papyri*, 1231.56. This text is from Bowra's *Greek Lyric Poetry*.
Bowra adds a few letters to Page's text. The version in my
Greek Lyric Poetry was based on Edmonds' restored text,
and so it is very different:

> Happy groom, we virgins at your door
> will pass the night singing of the love
> between you and your bride. Her breasts
> are like sweet violets.
>
> With the rays of dawn wake and leave,
> and let the great god Hermes lead you
> where dog days will not come — no more
> than will our sleep tonight.

This song sung by girls outside the window of the newly-
weds humorously tells the groom to awaken and go out and
join his old friends. The taunting tone goes well with the
happiness of the occasion.

[54] From a third-century papyrus, *Oxyrhynchus Papyri*, 1232.1. i. 8–9.

[55] Himerios, *Epithalamy of Severus*, 1.20, writes: "And
if an ode were needed, I would give a song such as this:
[paraphrase of poem follows]." The Greek text is the prose
paraphrase.

[56] Dionysios, *On Literary Composition*, 25.

[57] Hephaistion, *Handbook of Meter*, 107, and Chori-
cius, *Epithalamy of Zachary*, 97. There are sharp differences in text and interpretation in Edmonds, Diehl, Bowra,
and Page. The most coherent text is in Edmonds. Catullus
has phrases reminiscent of these lines: *mellitos oculos*
(48.1) and *Pulcher es, neque te Venus neglegit* (61.194).

[58] Demetrios, *On Style*, 148, writes: "There is a charm
peculiarly Sapphic in its way when having said something,
she changes her mind, as [poem follows], as if interrupting
herself because she has resorted to an impossible hyperbole, for no one really is as tall as Ares."

[59] Athenaios, *Doctors at Dinner*, 10.425 c, writes: "According to some versions the wine-bearer of the gods was Harmonia. Alkaios makes Hermes also the wine-bearer, as does Sappho in the following: [poem follows]."

[60] Hephaistion, *Handbook of Meter*, 27, and Servius on Virgil's *Georgics*, 1.31.

[61] Hephaistion, *Handbook of Meter*, 45. Synesios in *Letters*, 3.158 d, writes: "The man who is wronged is Harmonios, the father of the Head Doorkeeper, who, as Sappho would say, though in other respects he lived soberly and honestly, he claimed to be better born than Kekrops himself." For further reference to the doorkeeper who is mocked in this song, see *Testimonia*.

[62] Chrysippos, *Negatives*, col. 14.23.

[63] Libanios, *Orations*, i 402, writes: "If nothing prevented Sappho the Lesbian from wishing that the length of her night be doubled, then I may make a similar prayer." From this Edmonds suggests Sappho's words.

[64] Hephaistion, *Handbook of Meter*, 68.

[65] Himerios, *Epithalamy of Severus*, I, writes: "Come then, we will lead our discourse into the bridal chamber and introduce it to the beauty of the bride. O beautiful and charming, these are the Lesbian's praises for you. Your playmates are the roseate-ankled Graces and golden Aphrodite, and the seasons make the meadows bloom." From these words of Himerios Edmonds construes the Greek text.

[66] Demetrios, *On Style*, 44 (see *Testimonia*).

[67] Apollonios, *Conjunctions*, 223.25.

[68] From a third-century papyrus, *Oxyrhynchus Papyri*, 1232.1. i. 8–9. The poem ends with Σαπφοῦς μελῶν β′ "End of the Second Book of Sappho's Poems." The text here is as restored by Hunt, Wilamowitz, Lobel, and Edmonds; in some places the reading of Lobel-Page is followed. This hymeneal song, from the book of epithalamia, is more narratively epic and Homeric in word and idea than any other existing fragment of Sappho. Because of these qualities not normally found in Sappho, Page cast some doubt as to her authorship.

[69] From a seventh-century manuscript, *Berliner Klas-*

sikertexte, P. 9722.5. This fragment appears as a continuation of E. 86, D. 98, LP 96. The restoration by Edmonds is extensive.

[70] Julian, *Letter to Iamblichus,* 60.

[71] Maximus of Tyre, *Dissertations,* 24(18).9 (see *Testimonia*).

[72] Hephaistion, *Handbook of Meter,* 87.

[73] Athenaios, *Doctors at Dinner,* 1.21 b.

[74] Herodian, *Words without Parallel,* 2.932.23 Lentz.

[75] Aldus, *Cornucopia,* 286 b.

[76] Priscian, *Grammar,* 2.77. Keil. Bergk and Edmonds assign this fragment to Sappho; Diehl and Page to Alkaios.

[77] Athenaios, *Doctors at Dinner,* 13.571 d (fr. 12) see *Niobe* in *Glossary*).

[78] Hephaistion, *Handbook of Meter,* 72. Where Edmonds has ὄρρανα, Diehl has Ὠ<ι>ραν<ν>α and Page Ὤιρανα, both proper nouns.

[79] Scholiast on Pindar, *O.*2.96. The second half of the fragment may be the commentator's gloss.

[80] Stobaios, *Anthology,* 4.12, writes: "Sappho to a woman of no education."

[81] Athenaios, *Doctors at Dinner,* 13.56 d, writes: "And Sappho also says to the man who is excessively admired for his beauty: [poem follows]."

[82] Hephaistion, *Handbook of Meter,* 44. Aristotle, *Rhetoric,* 1.9, writes: "We are ashamed of what is shameful, whether it is said, done or intended; compare Sappho's answer when Alkaios said: 'I want to speak to you but shame disarms me.'" Edmonds assigns part one to Alkaios and part two to Sappho. Diehl and Page assign the first line of part one to Alkaios and the remaining lines to Sappho. The text in all cases is substantially the same.

[83] Galenos, *Exhortation to Learning,* 8, writes: "Since we know that the time of youth is like spring flowers and its pleasures do not last long, it is better to praise the Lesbian poet: [poem follows]."

[84] From a second-century papyrus, *Oxyrhynchus Papyri,* 1231.15. Text is from Edmonds 1st edition, 1922.

[85] *Etymologicum Magnum,* 485.45.

[86] From a second-century papyrus, *Oxyrhynchus Papyri*, 1231.9. The poem is restored by Edmonds.

[87] Chrysippos, *Negatives*, col. 8, fr. 13.

[88] Scholiast on Pindar, 4.410, writes: "He calls it [the Golden Fleece] immortal because it was of gold and gold is indestructible; compare Sappho: [his paraphrase follows]." Edmonds' reading is based on the Scholiast's paraphrase of Sappho. The Scholiast on Hesiod ascribes these lines to Pindar.

[89] Scholiast on Aristophanes, *Peace*, 1174, writes: "For the Lydian dyes differ . . . and Sappho states: [her lines follow]." *Three times* is derived from context.

[90] Pollux, *Vocabulary*, 7.73.

[91] Scholiast on Apollonios of Rhodes, *Argonautika*, 1.727.

[92] Herodianos, *Words without Parallel*, 2.945.8 Lentz.

[93] Gregorios on Hermogenes, 7.1236 Walz (E. 61).

Demetrios, *On Style*, 161 (E. 59, 60), writes: "The charm of comedy lies especially in hyperbole, and each hyperbole is an impossibility . . . such as Sappho's: [phrases follow]."

Athenaios, *Doctors at Dinner*, 2.57 d (E. 62).

[94] Demetrios, *On Style*, 146. Diehl and Lobel-Page are followed here. Edmonds combines D. 115, and D. 123.

[95] Athenaios, *Doctors at Dinner*, 15.674 d, writes: "Sappho gives a more simple reason for wearing garlands: [her lines follow] in which she urges all who offer sacrifice to wreathe their heads, since being adorned with flowers makes them more pleasing to the gods."

[96] Hephaistion, *Handbook of Meter*, 69.

[97] Aristides, *Orations*, 2.932.29 Lentz.

[98] Plutarch, *On Restraining Anger*, 7, writes: "A man who is silent over his wine is boring and vulgar, and in anger there is nothing more dignified than tranquility, as Sappho advises [her lines follow]." Sappho gives her advice in the second person imperative. In this translation the advice is given in the first person singular.

[99] Philon, *On Punishment*, in a third-century papyrus, *Oxyrhynchus Papyri*, 1356.4 a. 14, writes: ". . . yielding to

the good counsel of the woman poet Sappho." The poem
follows.

[100] Aristides, *Orations*, 1.425, writes: "The glow which
is upon the whole city, not as Sappho said, blinding the
eyes, but . . . nor indeed as she said, like a hyacinth, but
. . ." Edmonds extracts these lines from the *Orations*. The
text here is not from Edmonds' *Lyra Graeca* but from his
Sappho in the Added Light of the New Fragments (Cambridge, 1912), p. 25.

[101] Herodian, *On Inflections*, 2.187.16.

[102] Apollonios, *Pronouns*, 66.3. Lobel-Page, 129, includes both E. 22 and E. 124, or D. 18 and D. 146.

[103] Julian, *Letter to Eugenius*, 18, writes: "I would
fly to the very foot of your mountains to embrace you, my
darling, as Sappho says."

[104] *Etymologicum Magnum*, 335.38. Page and Diehl
include in D. 14 and L.P. 37 both E. 17 and E. 18. Diehl
and Page read ἄνεμοι where Edmonds read ἄνοαι, which
changes the meaning of the entire fragment.

[105] Klearchos in Athenaios, *Doctors at Dinner*, 12.554
b, writes: "All lovers ripe with passion are attracted to
beautiful things. For it is natural that those who believe
themselves to be beautiful and blooming find it natural to
gather flowers. That is why Persephone's companions are
described as gathering flowers and Sappho says that she
saw a very beautiful girl picking flowers." Edmonds takes
his text from Klearchos' paraphrase.

[106] Herodianos, *Words without Parallel*, 2.932.29
Lentz. There are many variant readings of this fragment.

[107] *Etymologicum Magnum*, 449.36.

[108] Diogenianos, *Centuries of Proverbs*, 1.279, writes:
[Sappho's lines] said of those who are unwilling to take the
sour with the sweet."

[109] Apollonios, *Pronouns*, 99.17; *Etymologicum Magnum*, 117.14.

[110] From a second-century papyrus, *Oxyrhynchus Papyri*, 1231-15. The last two lines of this text, restored by
Edmonds, were omitted. They begin a new thought.

[111] From a second-century papyrus, *Oxyrhynchus Papyri*, 1231-13. The fragment is restored quite differently by

Edmonds, Diehl, and Page (in *Sappho and Alcaeus*). Only the first of the two stanzas, about which there is more agreement, is included here.

[112] Hephaistion, *Handbook of Meter*, 98.

[113] From the oldest extant papyrus of Sappho and Alkaios, of the third century B.C., or a little later. The fragment is in Milan and was first published by Vogliano in *Philologus*, xciii, 1939, pp. 277 ff. For the material on the first part of the papyrus (a), see poem 3 and notes for 3. The free translation of the second stanza is based on Page's interpretation, *Sappho and Alcaeus*, p. 102. He suggests that line 6 refers to the tyrant Myrsilos.

[114] From a third-century papyrus, *Oxyrhynchus Papyri*, 1787.6. Mika may be a shortened form of her friend Mnasidika. The house of Penthilos may refer to a rival school (thiasos) or, more likely, a rival political party. Pittakos, the tyrant of Lesbos, married the sister of a former leader, Drakon, who was the son of Penthilos.

[115] From a third-century papyrus, *Oxyrhynchus Papyri* 7. Our text is from Page's *Sappho and Alcaeus*. This version differs from Lobel-Page in the partial restoration of line 7. The poem is to her brother Charaxos. The black torment is presumably his Egyptian mistress, Doricha, on whom Charaxos was "wasting" his fortune. In the very mutilated lines which follow (not included here) Sappho seems to broaden her attack on Doricha.

[116] From a second-century papyrus, *Oxyrhynchus Papyri*, 1231.1 i (a).

[117] From a third-century papyrus, *Oxyrhynchus Papyri*, 1787, fr. 1+2. Commenting on the last lines of the poem, Athenaios in *Doctors at Dinner*, 15.687 a, writes: "So you think that refinement without virtue is desirable? But Sappho, who was a real woman and poet, was loath to separate good from refinement, saying: 'Yet I love refinement, and beauty and light/ are for me the same as desire for the sun.' It thus is clear that the desire to live included for Sappho both the bright and the good, and these belong to virtue."

[118] From a third-century papyrus, *Oxyrhynchus Papyri*, 1787, fr. 3. col. 2. 15–24.

[119] From a third-century papyrus, *Oxyrhynchus Papyri*, 1787, fr. 3. col. 2. 3–14.

[120] *Palatine Anthology*, 7.505. Ascription to Sappho is unlikely.

[121] Hephaistion, *Handbook of Meter*, 69. Where Edmonds reads *peace* Diehl and other editors read a name, Iranna, or some variation of such a name.

[122] From a first-century papyrus, *Oxyrhynchus Papyri*, 220.9.

[123] Aristotle, *Rhetoric*, 2.23. Edmonds' text contains his metrical version. The Lobel-Page text, used here, records Aristotle's paraphrase.

[124] *Palatine Anthology*, 7.489. The ascription of this well-known poem to Sappho is not accepted by most recent scholars.

[125] R. Rainer, 29.777 a. The text is from Max Treu's edition of Sappho. Treu restores a few letters not found in Lobel-Page text. Here the Atreides is probably Menelaos.

[126] Lobel-Page assigns the poem to Alkaios but Max Treu strongly defends it as Sappho's. He cites the line "I shall always be a virgin" as Sappho's speech and rejects as insufficient the Page argument based on recurring forms. The single unintelligible words of the first and last lines of the Greek text are omitted here.

[127] *Etymologicum Magnum*, 822.39. It is uncertain what flower the hyacinth was to the Greeks.

[128] Stobaios, *Anthology*, 71.4, writes: "In marriage it is best to consider the ages of the people concerned. Sappho writes: [her lines follow]."

[129] Maximus of Tyre, *Dissertations*, 24 (18) .9, writes: "Diotima says (in Plato's *Symposium*) that love flowers in prosperity and dies in want." Sappho put these together and called it bittersweet [see poem 25] and giver of pain. While Sokrates calls love sophistical, Sappho calls it a weaver of tales.

[130] Apollonios, *Pronouns*, 66.3.

[131] Apollonios, *Pronouns*, 98.2.

[132] Demetrios, *On Style*, 141, writes: "Sappho also creates charm from the use of anaphora, as in this passage about the Evening Star: [her lines follow]. Here the charm

ies in the repetition of the word *bring*." In *Don Juan*, iii.
107, Byron imitated Sappho:

> O Hesperus, thou bringest all good things —
> Home to the weary, to the hungry cheer,
> To the young bird the parent's brooding wings,
> The welcome stall to the o'erlaboured steer;
> Whate'er of peace about our hearthstone clings,
> Whate'er our household gods protect of dear,
> Are gathered round us by thy look of rest;
> Thou bring'st the child too to its mother's breast.

[133] From a seventh-century manuscript, *Berliner Klassikertexte* P 9722.4. The text used follows the equivalent
of lines 6–13 of Lobel-Page text. The first and last lines are
either unintelligible or unrelated. Sappho is apparently re-
plying to a question from her friend Gongyla whose name,
by itself, appears in line 4, Lobel-Page.

[134] From a second-century papyrus, *Oxyrhynchus Papyri*, 1231.9. The fragment is very much restored.

[135] Maximus of Tyre, *Dissertations*, 18.9, writes:
"Sokrates reproves Xanthippe for crying when she is near
death as Sappho does her daughter: [her lines follow]."

[136] Aristides, *On the Extemporised Addition*, 2.508,
writes: "Sappho too once boasted to some women who
were thought to be wealthy that the Muses had given her
true happiness and good fortune and that when dead she
would not be forgotten." Edmonds devises his text from
Aristides' prose paraphrase of Sappho's words.

[137] Dio Chrysostom, *Discourses*, 37.47, writes: "'Someone I tell you, will remember us,' as Sappho has well said
. . . for we are oppressed by fears of oblivion, but always
saved by judgment of good men." E. 77, the second part of
text, is Edmonds' restoration based on Dio Chrysostom's
paraphrase.

[138] Scholiast on Sophokles' *Elektra*. This fragment,
included in *Lyra Graeca* (1940), vol. III., is ascribed to
Sappho or Alkaios.

[139] *Berliner Klassikertexte*, 5 P 5006. The Lobel-Page
text is followed except for line 7 where]λον is amended to
read κά]λον. The text is obviously fragmentary, scarcely
more than a column of words, yet the words are intelligible;

the syntax and connective words present the main difficulty
Ezra Pound's early poem, imitating Sappho, suggests a
similar scrap of papyrus:

PAPYRUS

Spring . . .

Too long . . .

Gongula . . .

[140] *Oxyrhynchus Papyri*, 1787. fr. 4. The problems of
the text are similar to those of 139. No new word in the
translation has been added apart from the connective *a*
in line 9. Where the Greek text has *Acheron*, the river of
death running through Hades, I have used *Hades*.

[141] Strabon, *Geography*, 1.40.

[142] *Oxyrhynchus Papyri*, 1231.15.11-12.

[143] *Old Etymologicum Magnum*, Miller p. 213.

[144] Apollonios, *Pronouns*, 82.16.

[145] *Oxyrhynchus Papyri*, 1231.1. ii (a).

[146] Apollonios, *On Pronouns*, 93.23.

[147] Apollonios, *Pronouns*, 93.23.

[148] Pollux, *Vocabulary*, 6.107, writes: "Anakreon . . .
says that dill was used for garlands, as Sappho and Alkaios
also said. The two latter also speak of celery." From Pollux,
Edmonds suggests "garlands of celery."

[149] Apollonios, *Pronouns*, 107.11.

[150] Zenobios, Centuries of Proverbs, writes: " 'She
loves children even more than Gello does,' a saying for
those who die young or of those whose loving indulgence of
children spoils them. For Gello was a virgin who died
young, and the Lesbians say that her ghost haunts little
children, and they ascribe to her the death of young
children."

[151] Hephaistion, *Handbook of Meter*, 89.

[152] *Etymologicum Magnum*, 759.35.

[153] Scholiast on Aristophanes, 729.

[154] From a Paris manuscript, edited by Cramer, *Inedita*
(Oxford) 1.71.19.

[155] *Etymologicum Magnum*, 174.42.

[156] Pollox, *Vocabulary*, 6.98.

[157] Marius Plotius, *Art of Grammar*, 6.516 Keil.

[158] Marius Plotius, *Art of Grammar*, 6.517 Keil.

TESTIMONIA

Including the chief references in Greek and Latin prose and poetry to Sappho and to her poetry; the order is roughly biography, encomia and other comment, literary criticism, indirect poems, prosody, from Greek poetry, from Latin poetry. For additional references to Sappho see quotations from grammarians and commentators in the *Sources and Notes.*

BIOGRAPHICAL

Sappho was the daughter, some say, of Simon or Eunominos or Eurygyos or Ekrytos or Semos or Skamon or Euarchos or Skamandronymos. Her mother's name was Kleïs. She was a Lesbian from Eresos and a lyric poet. She wrote in the 42d Olympiad, 612–609 B.C. together with Alkaios, Stesichoros and Pittakos. She had three brothers, Larichos, Charaxos and Eurygyos, and married Kerkolas, a very rich man from Andros and had a daughter by him named Kleïs. She had three companions and friends, Atthis, Telesippa and Megara, to whom she was slanderously accused of being attached in a shameful love. Her disciples were Anagora of Miletos, Gongyla of Kolophon, and Euneika of Salamis. She wrote nine books of lyric poetry and invented the quill for playing the lyre. She wrote epigrams, iambic poems and monodies.

The Suda Lexicon, a

The poet Sappho, daughter of Skamandronymos. Even Plato, son of Ariston, calls her wise and skillful. I understand that there was also another Sappho of Lesbos who was a courtesan, not a poet.

Aelian, Historical Miscellanies, 12.19.

Sappho was born on the island of Lesbos and lived in the city of Mytilene. Her father was Skamandros or according to some Skamandronymos. She had three brothers, Eurygyos, Larichos, and Charaxos who was the oldest. The latter went to Egypt and became the lover of Doricha on whom he spent a great deal of money. Since Larichos was the youngest, Sappho loved him most. She also had a daughter Kleïs, named after her own mother. She was accused by some writers of being irregular in her way of life and a woman-lover. Her looks seem to have been contemptible and terribly ugly. She had a dark complexion and was very short. . . . She uses the (Aiolic) dialect, and has written (nine) books of lyric poetry and one of elegiac and. . . .

Oxyrhynchus Papyri, 1800.1.1.

The beautiful Sappho. Sokrates liked to call her this because of the beauty of her song, although she was small and dark.

Maximus of Tyre, 24.18.7

Physically, Sappho was very ugly, small and dark, and one can only describe her as a nightingale with deformed wings enfolding a tiny body.

Scholiast on Lucian Portraits, 18

Sappho, a lyric poet, daughter of Skamandronymos and a native of Mytilene.

Scholiast on Plato's Phaidros, 235 c

From Eresos came Theophrastos and Phanias the peripatetic Philosophers.*

Strabon, Geography, 13.617

---

* Had Strabon thought Sappho to have been born in Eresos it is probable that he would have included her name in this list.

The renowned poets Sappho and Alkaios lived in the Olympiad 45.2 (598 B.C.).

Eusebios, Chronicle

From the time Sappho went from Mytilene to Sicily when she was exiled (603–595 – perhaps for the second time). This was when Kritias the younger was ruling Athens and during the rule of Gamori (landowners) at Syracuse. (598 B.C.)

Parian Chronicle, 36

Here Hermesianax is wrong in making Sappho a contemporary of Anakreon. For he belongs to the time of Cyrus and Polykrates while Sappho is a contemporary of Alyattes, father of Kroisos.

Athenaios, Doctors at Dinner, 599 c

Sappho was a Lesbian from Mytilene and a lyre player. She threw herself down from the Leukadian Cliff out of love for Phaon of Mytilene. Some say that she was also a lyric poet.

The Suda Lexicon, b

You are a Phaon both in beauty and deeds. This proverb is used for those who are handsome and proud. They say that Sappho among many others, was in love with Phaon but she was not the poet Sappho but another Lesbian, who, having failed in winning his love, leapt from the Leukadian Cliff.

The Suda Lexicon: Phaon

Phaon, a ferryman who made his living sailing back and forth between Lesbos and the mainland, one day took Venus in the guise of an old woman over for nothing. She gave him an alabaster box of unguents which he used daily to make women fall in love with him. Among them was one who in her frustration was said to have jumped from Mount Leukates, and from this story came the present custom of hiring people once a year to jump into the sea from that place.

Servius on the Aeneid, 10.452

The temple of Apollo Leukates also has a ledge from which one can cure love. Menandros says, "Sappho was the first to leap from the prominent rock in her amorous pursuit of the proud Phaon. But in accordance with my vow I shall praise your sacred precinct on the Leukadian cliff, O Lord Apollo." Although Menandros assigns Sappho priority in jumping, the older authorities say it was Kephalos who was in love with Pterelas, son of Deioneus. It was an annual custom of the Leukadians to throw some guilty person from the cliff during the sacrifice to Apollo in order to avert further evil; they tied all kinds of birds and winged creatures to him so that they might brake his fall by their fluttering, and a large crowd waited for him underneath in small boats to save him, if possible, in that area outside the sacred precinct.

Strabon, *Geography*, 10.452

It is said that this pyramid was built by her lovers as a tomb for a courtesan who is called Doricha by the lyric poet Sappho when she became the mistress of Sappho's brother Charaxos when he visited Naukratis with a cargo of Lesbian wine; others call her Rhodopis.

Strabon, *Geography*, 17.808

There are people in Greece who say that this pyramid was erected by the courtesan Rhodopis. They are quite wrong, and I do not think they even know who Rhodopis was. . . . She was born a Thracian, the slave of Iadmon, son of Hephaistopolis of Samos, a fellow slave of Aisopos, the writer of fables.

She was brought to Egypt by Xantheus the Samian, to ply her trade, and Charaxos of Mytilene, son of Skamandronymos and brother of the poet Sappho, paid a large sum to redeem her from slavery. It seems that Naukratis must be a good place for beautiful prostitutes, for not only did Rhodopis live there and become so famous that every Greek was familiar with her name. . . . When Charaxos returned to Mytilene after setting Rhodopis free, he was ridiculed by Sappho in one of her poems.

Herodotos, *Histories*, 2.135

Naukratis produced some famous and outstandingly beautiful courtesans. Doricha became Charaxos' mistress when he went to Naukratis on a business trip, and beautiful Sappho accuses her in a poem of having fleeced her brother Charaxos of much of his fortune. But Herodotos calls her Rhodopis (instead of Doricha) but he does not know that she is not the same woman who dedicated the famous spits at Delphi which Kratinos mentions. The following epigram was written by Poseidippos, who speaks of her many times in the Aisopeia: "Doricha, your bones are covered now by only a headband for your soft hair and also by the perfumed robe in which you once wrapped your graceful Charaxos while embracing him until it was time for the morning wine. But the white speaking pages of Sappho's song still remain. Blessed is your name which Naukratis will preserve as long as any ship sails the shallow Nile."

Another beautiful courtesan was Archedike of Naukratis. According to Nymphis in his *Voyage Around Asia*, the courtesan of Eresos who was a namesake of the other Sappho became famous as the lover of beautiful Phaon.

Athenaios, *Doctors at Dinner*, 13.596 b

If it is right to argue from one age to another, the Lesbian's love was nothing else but that which Sokrates practiced. Both seem to me to have engaged in the same kind of friendships, she of women, he of men, and both said that they could fall in love many times and all beautiful people attracted them. What Alkibiades, Charmides and Phaidros were to him, Gyrinna, Atthis and Anaktoria were to her; and what his rival philosophers, Prodikos, Gorgias, Thrasymachos and Protagoras were to Sokrates, so Gorgo and Andromeda were to Sappho, who sometimes rebuked them, at others refuted them and spoke ironically about them just as Sokrates did about his rivals. For example, Sokrates says, "Good morning, Ion," and Sappho begins a poem with, "A very bright good morning, Andromeda — O daughter from kings and sons of kings."

Maximus of Tyre, *Dissertations*, 24 (18). 9

The grammarian Didymus wrote four thousand books. I would pity anyone who simply had to read so many supremely empty works. Among his books he enquires about the birthplace of Homer, the real mother of Aeneas, whether Anakreon was more of a lecher than a drunkard, whether Sappho was a prostitute, and other things which you ought to forget if you knew them. And then people complain that life is short.

Seneca, *Letters to Lucilius*. Ep. 88

And do you think that refinement without virtue is desirable? Why Sappho, who was a true woman and a poet, had too much reverence to separate honor from refinement, for she says: "Yet I love refinement, and the bright and the beautiful are for me the same as desire for sunlight." She made it clear to all that her desire for living included both the bright and the honorable. For these belong to virtue.

Athenaios, *Doctors at Dinner*, 15.687

It was the custom among the ancient peoples for the young men of the noblest families to serve the wine . . . Beautiful Sappho often praises her brother Larichos for the way he served the wine in the council hall of Mytilene.

Athenaios, *Doctors at Dinner*, 10.424 e

Sokrates: There are wise people from earlier times who wrote and spoke of these things and would take exception if I agreed with you. *Phaidros:* Who are they? What have they said that is better? *Sokrates:* I cannot say offhand but it is clear that I got better information from one of the ancients, either from the beautiful Sappho or the wise Anakreon or some historian.

Plato, *Phaidros*, 235 b

Sokrates rebukes Xanthippe for crying when he is about to die, as does Sappho her daughter, when she writes: "It would be wrong for us. It is not right for mourning to enter a home of poetry."

Maximus of Tyre, *Dissertations*, 24.18.9

ENCOMIA AND OTHER COMMENT

The sweet glory of the Lesbians.

Lucian, *Loves*, 30

A contemporary of Pittakos and Alkaios was Sappho — a marvel. In all the centuries since history began we know of no woman who in any true sense can be said to rival her as a poet.

Strabon, *Geography*, 13.617

One evening, while drinking wine, the nephew of Solon the Athenian sang one of Sappho's songs, and Solon liked it so much that he ordered the boy to teach it to him. When one of the company asked why he was learning it, he answered, "I want to learn it before I die."

Stobaios, *Anthology*, Fl. 29.28

Everybody honors the wise. The Parians honored Archilochos despite his slanderous tongue, the Chians honored Homer though he was not a Chian, and the Mytilineans honored Sappho although she was a woman.

Aristotle, *Rhetoric*, 1398 b

"Don't you see," he said, "what charm the songs of Sappho have to hold the listeners spellbound?

Plutarch, *Pythian Oracles*, 6

We were the first to be displeased with and condemn the new custom, which was imported into Rome, of reading from Plato as an after-dinner entertainment and listening to his dialogues over the dessert, perfumes and wine, so that now when they recite Sappho or Anakreon I think I should put down my cup out of shame.

Plutarch, *Dinner-Table Problems*, 7.8.2

It is fitting to mention Sappho along with the Muses. The Romans speak of how Kakos, son of Hephaistos, let fire and flames flow out of his mouth. And Sappho's words are truly mixed with fire, and through her songs she brings out her heart's warmth, and according to Philoxenos heals the pain of love with the sweet-voiced Muse.

Plutarch, Amatorius, 18

After eating, it was time for wine and conversation, Antonius Julianus desired that we might have a performance by excellent singers of both sexes whom he knew our young friend had at his disposal. And then young men and women were presented to us and they sang in a pleasant way many songs by Anakreon and Sappho and also some erotic elegies by recent composers.

Aulus Gellius, Attic Nights, 19.3

For these ladies consider it the highest kind of embellishment when people say that they are educated and wise and write poems almost as good as Sappho's.

Lucian, On Paid Companions, 36

The Mytileneans engraved Sappho on their coins.

Pollux, Vocabulary, 9.84

And now freeborn women and virgins call their intimate friends *hetairai* as Sappho does in this passage: "On this day I will sing beautifully and make you happy, dear comrades." (*see* poem 13)

Athenaios, Doctors at Dinner, 13.571 d

The statue of Sappho stolen from the town hall of Syracuse. . . . Not only was it beautifully done but it contained a famous epigram on the base.

Cicero, Orations against Verres, 2.4.57

LITERARY CRITICISM

My children, since we are now calling upon our Muses to come to the dance and love-making of marriage, it is now time for us to end the solemn music and begin to dance with the virgins and so honor Aphrodite. It is very hard to find a pleasant enough song to please the goddess. We judge this from the poets themselves who, though skilled in love poetry, when it comes to writing poems about Hera, are as brave as young men and women. But the rites of Aphrodite they leave to the Lesbian Sappho who sings to the lyre and writes the epithalamium. She enters the room after the contest among the suiters, weaves the bower, makes the bridal bed, brings the virgins into the bridal chamber and brings Aphrodite in her car drawn by Graces and a band of Cupids, her playmates. She braids Aphrodite's hair with hyacinth, except for the locks near her forehead which she leaves free to float and wave in the breezes. Then she adorns the curls of the Cupids with gold, and she places them before the car in order that they may wave their torches high.

Himerios, *Orations*, 1.4

For a second and third example we may think of Theano and the Lesbian poet, and for a fourth, Diotima. Theano contributed an idea of greatness of mind and Sappho gave us refinement.

Lucian, *Portraits*, 18

Anakreon of Teos was the first poet after Sappho of Lesbos to make love the main subject of his poetry.

Pausanias, *Descriptions of Greece*, 1.25.1

In his second book of *Erotika*, Klearchos says that the love songs and Lokrian verse of Gnesippos are not different from the poems of Sappho or Anakreon.

Athenaios, *Doctors at Dinner*, 13.605 e

We forgive the unmeasured and excessive praises given by Sappho and Anakreon to their beloved.

                                    Themistios, *Orations*, 13, p. 170 d

The Mixolydian mode is especially passionate, befitting tragedy. Aristoxenos declares that this mode was invented by Sappho and that the writers of tragedy learned from her.

                                    Plutarch, *On Music*, 16

This talented woman's name was Damophyla, and it is said that she had virgin girl friends, just as Sappho did, and that she composed love poems and hymns as Sappho did. The hymns to Artemis are derived ultimately from Sapphic models.

                              Philostratos, *Life of Apollonios of Tyana*, 1.30

Then comes the polished and decorative style which prefers elegance to solemnity. It uses the smoothest and gentlest words, seeking euphony and musicality from which comes its charm. It does not let words come together by chance or thoughtlessly but it places each word carefully with another to reproduce the most musical effect; it is concerned with the general arrangement that will produce the most graceful combination; it attempts to put things together with regard to the coherence of the parts and the perfection of the union of these parts. . . . These seem to me to be the characteristics of this style. Examples of this style are Hesiod, Sappho and Anakreon in poetry, and in prose the Athenian Isokrates and members of his school.

                           Dionysios of Halikarnassos, *Demosthenes*, 40

The finished and florid composition has the following characteristics. . . . It would be pertinent for me to enumerate the people who excelled in it. Among the epic poets Hesiod seems to me to have best worked out this style, and among the lyrical poets, Sappho; and with her, Anakreon and Simonides; among the tragic poets, only Euripides; among the historians, no one, to be exact but Ephoros and

Theopompos somewhat more than the others; among the orators, Isokrates. I shall now give examples of this style, using Sappho for the poets and Isokrates for the orators. I begin with the poet: [There follows the complete poem "A Prayer to Aphrodite."] The verbal beauty and charm of this passage lie in the cohesion and smoothness of the connecting phrases. For the words follow each other and are woven according to the natural affinities and unions of the syllables.

> Dionysios of Halikarnassos, *Literary Composition*, 23

For example Sappho takes the emotions appropriate to the passion of love from true life. And she shows her virtue when she takes the best and most excellent events and expertly selects and combines them. [There follows the poem "Seizure."] Is it not wonderful how simultaneously she summons the soul, body, hearing, tongue, sight, flesh, all as separate things distinct from herself, and by contrary elements, she both freezes and burns, is mad and sane, she is afraid or she is nearly dead; thus not only one passion is evident but a whole assembly of emotions; for all these things happen to lovers, and her taking the best of the emotions, as I said, and joining them together, produces the excellence of this passage.

> Longinus, *The Sublime*, 10

There are many kinds of literary charm. But, first, charm may be in the subject, as, for example, subjects such as gardens of the nymphs, a wedding, a love affair, which is found in all the poetry of Sappho.

> Demetrios, *On Style*, 132

In a different way Sappho makes fun of the rustic bridegroom and the doorkeeper of the bridal chamber. It is a very commonplace style, pertaining more to prose than to poetry, and so it would be better for these poems to be spoken rather than to be sung. They are not suitable for the dance or the lyre unless for a kind of dance-argument.

> Demetrios, *On Style*, 167

The charm that comes from her use of formal devices is evident and frequent, such as the use of repetition where the bride says to her virginity: "Virginity, virginity, when you leave me, where do you go?" And she replies with the same formal device: "I am gone and never come back to you. I never return." For more grace is evident than if it had been said only once and this formal device had not been used. And although repetition seems to have been invented in order to show force, Sappho even uses what is very forceful with great charm.

Demetrios, On Style, 140

And therefore when Sappho sings of beauty she is sweet and full of beautiful words, and the same holds true when she sings of love, spring and the halcyon; and every beautiful word is woven into her poetry, some of which she invented herself.

Demetrios, On Style, 166

INDIRECT POEMS

Sappho loves the rose and always crowns it with praise, comparing the beautiful virgins to it; and she compares it to the arms of the Graces when they have left them bare.

Philostratos, Letters, 51

For Homer says that she [Niobe] had six [children] of each sex, Euripides seven, Sappho nine, and Bakchylides and Pindar ten. (See Niobe in Glossary and poem 77.)

Gellius, Attic Nights, 20.7

Some take this to mean that Theseus set free seven boys and seven girls, as Plato says in the Phaidon, Sappho in her lyric poems, Bakchylides in his dithyrambs and Euripides in his Herakles.

Servius on Virgil's Aeneid, 6.21

After Prometheus created man, he is said to have ascended to heaven with Minerva's help, and there lighting a torch on the sun's wheel, he stole the fire and revealed it to man. The gods being angered by this sent two evils upon the earth, fever (or women) and disease, as we are told by Sappho and Hesiod.

Servius on Virgil's *Eclogues*, 6.42

Sappho sang many contradictory things about love.

Pausanias, *Description of Greece*, 9.27.3

Alkaios called Eros the son of Iris and Zephyros; Sappho called him the son of Aphrodite and Ouranos.

Scholiast on Theokritos, 13.1/2 c

Sappho said that Eros descended from Ge [Earth] and Ouranos.

Scholiast on Apollonios of Rhodes, 3.26

And it is said that Selene [the moon] goes down in that cave to meet Endymion. Sappho and Nikandros, in his book on Europa, relate the love of Selene.

Scholiast on Apollonios of Rhodes, *Argonautika*, 4.57

Diotima says (in Plato's *Symposium*) that love flowers in prosperity and dies in want. Sappho put these together and called him bittersweet. (See poems 25, 129.)

Maximus of Tyre, *Dissertations*, 24 (180.9)

The *baromos* and *barbitos*, mentioned by both Sappho and Anakreon, and the trigonon (triangles) and *sambuka* are all ancient instruments.

Athenaios, *Doctors at Dinner*, 4.182 e

Later the actual promontory seems to have been known as Aiga, as Sappho calls it, and later as Kane and Kanai.

Strabon, *Geography*, 13.615

These gifts of yours may be compared to the leader of the Muses himself, as Sappho and Pindar say in their odes when they adorn him with blond hair and a lyre, and give him a team of swans to dance with the Muses and Graces on Mt. Helikon; or when the poets inspired by the Muses lead the Bacchanal (so the lyre song calls Dionysos) in the first stirring of spring, and lead him with spring flowers and ivy to the peaks of the Caucasus and the valleys of Lydia, to the cliffs of Parnassos and the rock of Delphi, while he dances about and plays the Evian melody to the women who follow him.

Himerios, *Orations*, 13.7

Anakreon says that anise was used for making garlands, and so do Sappho and Alkaios, and the latter also speak of celery. (See poems 95, 148.)

Pollux, *Vocabulary*, 6.107

Sappho calls Zeus the holder [Hektor].

Hesychios, *Glossary*

Sappho calls the coffer in which unguents and woman's articles are kept γρύταν.

Phrynichos, *Introduction to Learning*, 1.34.2

Sappho's word βεῦδος is equivalent to κιμβερικόν, a transparent vest.

Pollux, *Vocabulary*, 7.9

θάψος is a wood called, in Sappho's word, Scytharium wood, and is used for dyeing.

Scholiast on Theokritos, 2.88

Pamphos, who composed the oldest hymns for the Athenians, called Linos by the name of Oitolinos (Dead Linos) at the climax of mourning for him. Sappho of Lesbos, having learned the name Oitolinos from the verses of Pamphos, sang of Adonis and Oitolinos together.

Pausanias, *Description of Greece*, 9.29.8

PROSODY

Menaichmos of Sikyon in his *Treatise on Artists* declares that Sappho was the first to use the *pectis* or quill.

> Athenaios, *Doctors at Dinner*, 14, 635 e

Chamaileon in his treatise *On Sappho*.

> Athenaios, *Doctors at Dinner*, 13, 599 c

Drakon of Stratonikeia, grammarian . . . who wrote *On Sappho's Meters*.

> *The Suda Lexicon*

First, the epichoriambias, also called the Sapphic eleven-syllable verse. . . . It also is found in Alkaios but it is not clear which of the two poets invented the verse, though it is named after Sappho.

> Hephaistion, *Handbook of Meter*, 43

The Sapphic variety of the heroic hexameter is a line which both begins and ends with a spondee. . . .

> Scholiast on Hephaistion's *Handbook of Meter*, 293, Cons.

You have given the *Geography* a literary distinction by prefixing it with the kind of iambic verses . . . which the beautiful Sappho chooses to go with her songs.

> Julian, *Letters, To Alypios*, 30

Poems are called common when they are formed of metrical systems in which the lines are of the same meter, such as in the second and third books of Sappho. In these the stanzas are two lines each and similar.

> Hephaistion, *Handbook on Poems*, 60

The dactylic Adonian dimeter catalectic was invented by Sappho, and for this reason it is also called the mono-schematist Sapphic, for it always consists of a dactyl and a spondee.

> Marius Plotius, *Art of Grammar*, 6.516 Keil

FROM GREEK POETRY

This tomb contains the silent bones of Sappho, but her wise sayings are immortal.

Pinytos, Palatine Anthology, 7.6

When you come by my Aiolian tomb, O stranger, do not speak of me, the singer of Mytilene, as dead. This tomb was made by human hands and such mortal works fall quickly into oblivion. But if you compare me to the sacred Muses from each of whom I took one flower for my nine books, you will know that I have escaped from the darkness of death, and that every day of sun keeps alive the name of the lyric poet Sappho.

Tullius Laureas, Palatine Anthology, 7.17

The flowers of Sappho, few but roses.

Meleagros' proem, Palatine Anthology, 4.1

My name is Sappho. My song surpasses the song of women as Homer's the song of men.

Antipatros of Sidon, Palatine Anthology, 7.15

Memory was astounded when she heard the honey-voiced Sappho, and she wondered whether mankind had a tenth Muse.

Antipatros of Sidon, Palatine Anthology, 9.66

Aiolian land, you cover Sappho, sung as a mortal Muse among the immortal Muses, whom Kypris and Eros educated. With Persuasion she wove the deathless wreath of the Pierian Muses. She was a joy to Greece and to you. Fates, you who twirl the three-ply thread on the distaff, why didn't you spin an eternal day for the singer who invented the enduring poems which were the gifts of the daughters of Helikon?

Antipatros of Sidon, Palatine Anthology, 7.14

Your poems are the sweetest pillow for young lovers. I am sure that Pieria or ivied Helikon must honor you, Sappho, and the Muses too, whose spirit you share, you the Muse of Aiolian Eresos. Hymen, the wedding god has you near when he stands with his bright torch by the bed of the newly-wed, or Aphrodite has you near when she laments the young offspring of Kinyras in the sacred grove of the blessed. At any rate, my lady, I greet you as a god, for your songs we think of as daughters of the immortals.

> Dioskorides on Sappho of Mytilene, the lyric poet, the marvel of lyric poetry.
> *Palatine Anthology*, 7.47

Sappho was the first to leap from the prominent rock in her amorous pursuit of the proud Phaon. But in accordance with my vow I shall praise your sacred precinct on the Leukadian cliff, O Lord Apollo.

> Menandros, quoted in Strabon, *Geography*, 10.452

Some say there are nine Muses. Count again. Behold the tenth: Sappho of Lesbos.

> Plato, *Palatine Anthology*, 9.506

Stranger, if you sail to Mytilene, the city of beautiful dances which kindled the fire of Sappho's beauty . . .

> Nossis, *Palatine Anthology*, 7.718

And you know how Alkaios the Lesbian played many songs on the lyre about his warm love for Sappho. He was a poet who loved the nightingale of song [Sappho], but he annoyed that other poet of Teos, Anakreon, because of his eloquence.

> Hermesianax in Athenaios, *Doctors at Dinner*, 598 b

The nine lyric poets. Learn the birthplace and ancestry of the foremost lyric poets and observe their fathers and their dialects. First was Alkaios from Mytilene, the honored musical son of Aiolos. And after him, from the same

land and dialect, came Sappho, daughter of Kleïs and
Eurygyos.

Scholiast on Pindar, i, 10

Doricha, your bones are covered now by only a headband for your soft hair and also by the perfumed robe in
which you once wrapped your graceful Charaxos while
embracing him until it was time for the morning wine. But
the white speaking pages of Sappho's song still remain.
Blessed is your name which Naukratis will preserve as long
as any ship sails the shallow Nile.

Poseidippos, *Aisopeia*, quoted in
Athenaios, *Doctors at Dinner*, 13.596 b

Painter, creative Nature herself gave you the Pierian
Muse from Mytilene to portray. Clarity is in her eyes and
this plainly reveals an imagination full of intelligence. Her
flesh is smooth and not painted unnaturally, and this shows
her simplicity. Mingled in her face are joy and the intel-
lectual spirit, showing the Muse joined with Kypris.

On a portrait of Sappho, Damochares,
Palatine Anthology, 16.30

Sappho's kisses would be sweet; sweet the embraces of
her snowy thighs and sweet all her body. But her soul is of
unyielding adamant. For her love stops at her lips and the
rest she keeps virgin. And who can stand this? Perhaps one
who could take this could easily endure the thirst of
Tantalos.

Paulus Silentiarius, *Palatine Anthology*, 5.246

Among Lesbian women with lovely locks of hair, Sappho
is the jewel.

Antipatros of Thessalonika, *Palatine Anthology*, 9.26

Fate granted you no small glory on the day you first saw
the light of the sun, Sappho, for we Muses agreed that your
words should be deathless, and the father of all, the thun-

derer, also concurred. You will be sung by all mortal men, and will not be poor in glorious fame.

> Anonymous, *Palatine Anthology*, 9.521

. . . but Sappho was not ninth among men but rather tenth among the lovely Muses.

> Anonymous, *Palatine Anthology*, 9.571

FROM LATIN POETRY

Sappho sang elegies to the girls of her city upon an Aiolian lyre, and you, Alkaios, sang more fully with a gold quill.

> Horace, Ode 2.13

The love still breathes, the flame is still alive that the Aiolian girl sang to her lyre.

> Horace, Ode 4.9.11

The manly Sappho adjusts her Muse to the meter of Archilochos.

> Horace, Epode 1.19.28

Girl more refined than the Sapphic Muse.

> Catullus, 35.16

What did Sappho teach other than how to love girls?

> Ovid, *Tristia*, 2.365

SAPPHO TO PHAON

Say, lovely youth that dost my heart command,
Can Phaon's eyes forget his Sappho's hand?
Must then her name the wretched writer prove,
To thy remembrance lost as to thy love?
  Ask not the cause that I new numbers choose,
The lute neglected and the lyric Muse:
Love taught my tears in sadder notes to flow,
And tuned my heart to elegies of woe.
  I burn, I burn, as when through ripened corn
By driving winds the spreading flames are borne.
Phaon to Aetna's scorching fields retires,
While I consume with more than Aetna's fires.
No more my soul a charm in music finds;
Music has charms alone for peaceful minds:
Soft scenes of solitude no more can please;
Love enters there and I'm my own disease.
No more the Lesbian dames my passion move,
Once the dear objects of my guilty love:
All other loves are lost in only thine,
Ah, youth ungrateful to a flame like mine!
Whom would not all those blooming charms surprise,
Those heavenly looks and dear deluding eyes?
The harp and bow would you like Phoebus bear,
A brighter Phoebus Phaon might appear:
Would you with ivy wreathe your flowing hair,
Not Bacchus' self with Phaon could compare:
Yet Phoebus loved, and Bacchus felt the flame;
One Daphne warmed and one the Cretan dame;
Nymphs that in verse no more could rival me
Than e'en those gods contend in charms with thee.
The Muses teach me all their softest lays,
And the wide world resounds with Sappho's praise.
Though great Alcaeus more sublimely sings
And strikes with bolder rage the sounding strings,

No less renown attends the moving lyre
Which Venus tunes and all her Loves inspire.
To me what Nature has in charms denied
Is well by wit's more lasting flames supplied.
Though short my stature, yet my name extends
To heaven itself and earth's remotest ends:
Brown as I am, an Aethiopian dame
Inspired young Perseus with a generous flame:
Turtles and doves of different hue unite,
And glossy jet is paired with shining white.
If to no charms thou wilt thy heart resign
But such as merit, such as equal thine,
By none, alas, by none thou canst be moved;
Phaon alone by Phaon must be loved.
Yet once thy Sappho could thy cares employ;
Once in her arms you centred all your joy:
No time the dear remembrance can remove,
For oh how vast a memory has love!
My music then you could for ever hear,
    And all my words were music to your ear:
You stopt with kisses my enchanting tongue,
And found my kisses sweeter than my song.
In all I pleased, but most in what was best;
And the last joy was dearer than the rest:
Then with each word, each glance, each motion fired
You still enjoyed, and yet you still desired,
Till all dissolving in the trance we lay
And in tumultuous raptures died away.
    The fair Sicilians now thy soul inflame:
Why was I born, ye gods, a Lesbian dame?
But ah, beware, Sicilian nymphs, nor boast
That wandering heart which I so lately lost;
Nor be with all those tempting words abused:
Those tempting words were all to Sappho used.
And you that rule Sicilia's happy plains,
Have pity, Venus, on your poet's pains.
    Shall fortune still in one sad tenor run
And still increase the woes so soon begun?
Inured to sorrow from my tender years,

My parent's ashes drank my early tears:
My brother next, neglecting wealth and fame,
Ignobly burned in a destructive flame:
An infant daughter late my griefs increased,
And all a mother's cares distract my breast.
Alas, what more could Fate itself impose,
But thee, the last and greatest of my woes?
No more my robes in waving purple flow,
Nor on my hand the sparkling diamonds glow;
No more my locks in ringlets curled diffuse
The costly sweetness of Arabian dews;
Nor braids of gold the varied tresses bind
That fly disordered with the wanton wind.
For whom should Sappho use such arts as these?
He's gone whom only she desired to please!
Cupid's light darts my tender bosom move;
Still is there cause for Sappho still to love;
So from my birth the Sisters fixed my doom,
And gave to Venus all my life to come:
Or, while my Muse in melting notes complains,
My yielding heart keeps measure to my strains.
By charms like thine, which all my soul have won,
Who might not — ah, who would not be undone?
For those, Aurora Cephalus might scorn,
And with fresh blushes paint the conscious morn:
For those, might Cynthia lengthen Phaon's sleep,
And bid Endymion nightly tend his sheep:
Venus for those had rapt thee to the skies,
But Mars on thee might look with Venus' eyes.
O scarce a youth, yet scarce a tender boy!
O useful time for lovers to employ!
Pride of thy age, and glory of thy race,
Come to these arms and melt in this embrace!
The vows you never will return, receive;
And take at least the love you will not give.
See, while I write, my words are lost in tears:
The less my sense, the more my love appears.
    Sure 'twas not much to bid one kind adieu:
At least, to feign was never hard to you.

"Farewell, my Lesbian love," you might have said;
Or coldly thus, "Farewell, O Lesbian maid."
No tear did you, no parting kiss receive,
Nor knew I then how much I was to grieve.
No lover's gift your Sappho could confer;
And wrongs and woes were all you left with her.
No charge I gave you, and no charge could give
But this, — "Be mindful of our loves, and live."
Now by the Nine, those powers adored by me,
And Love, the god that ever waits on thee; —
When first I heard (from whom I hardly knew)
That you were fled, and all my joys with you,
Like some sad statue, speechless, pale I stood;
Grief chilled my breast and stopt my freezing blood;
No sigh to rise, no tear had power to flow,
Fixed in a stupid lethargy of woe.
But when its way the impetuous passion found,
I rend my tresses and my breast I wound;
I rave, then weep; I curse, and then complain;
Now swell to rage, now melt in tears again.
Not fiercer pangs distract the mournful dame
Whose first-born infant feeds the funeral flame.
My scornful brother with a smile appears,
Insults my woes, and triumphs in my tears;
His hated image ever haunts my eyes; —
"And why this grief? thy daughter lives," he cries.
Stung with my love and furious with despair,
All torn my garments and my bosom bare,
My woes, thy crimes, I do the world proclaim;
Such inconsistent things are love and shame.
'Tis thou art all my care and my delight,
My daily longing and my dream by night. —
O night more pleasing than the brightest day,
When fancy gives what absence takes away,
And, dressed in all its visionary charms,
Restores my fair deserter to my arms!
Then round your neck in wanton wreath I twine;
Then you, methinks, as fondly circle mine:
A thousand tender words I hear and speak;

A thousand melting kisses give and take:
Then fiercer joys; I blush to mention these,
Yet, while I blush, confess how much they please.
But when with day the sweet delusions fly,
And all things wake to life and joy, but I;
As if once more forsaken, I complain,
And close my eyes to dream of you again:
Then frantic rise; and, like some fury, rove
Through lonely plains, and through the silent grove,
As if the silent grove and lonely plains,
That knew my pleasures, could relieve my pains.
I view the grotto, once the scene of love,
The rocks around, the hanging roofs above,
That charmed me more, with native moss o'ergrown,
Than Phrygian marble or the Parian stone:
I find the shades that veiled our joys before;
But, Phaon gone, those shades delight no more.
Here the pressed herbs with bending tops betray
Where oft entwined in amorous folds we lay;
I kiss that earth which once was pressed by you,
And all with tears the withering herbs bedew.
For thee the fading trees appear to mourn,
And birds defer their songs till thy return:
Night shades the groves, and all in silence lie, —
All but the mournful Philomel and I:
With mournful Philomel I join my strain;
Of Tereus she, of Phaon I complain.

A spring there is whose silver waters show,
Clear as a glass, the shining sands below:
A flowery lotos spreads its arms above,
Shades all the banks and seems itself a grove;
Eternal greens the mossy margin grace,
Watched by the sylvan genius of the place:
Here as I lay, and swelled with tears the flood,
Before my sight a watery virgin stood:
She stood and cried, — "O you that love in vain,
Fly hence and seek the fair Leucadian main:
There stands a rock from whose impending steep
Apollo's fane surveys the rolling deep;

There injured lovers, leaping from above,
Their flames extinguish and forget to love.
Deucalion once with hopeless fury burned;
In vain he loved, relentless Pyrrha scorned.
But when from hence he plunged into the main
Deucalion scorned, and Pyrrha loved in vain.
Haste, Sappho, haste, from high Leucadia throw
Thy wretched weight, nor dread the deeps below."

She spoke, and vanished with the voice: I rise,
And silent tears fall trickling from my eyes.
I go, ye nymphs, those rocks and seas to prove:
How much I fear, but ah, how much I love!
I go, ye nymphs, where furious love inspires;
Let female fears submit to female fires:
To rocks and seas I fly from Phaon's hate,
And hope from seas and rocks a milder fate.
Ye gentle gales, beneath my body blow,
And softly lay me on the waves below.
And thou, kind Love, my sinking limbs sustain,
Spread thy soft wings and waft me o'er the main,
Nor let a lover's death the guiltless flood profane.
On Phoebus' shrine my harp I'll then bestow,
And this inscription shall be placed below: —
"Here she who sung, to him that did inspire,
Sappho to Phoebus consecrates her lyre:
What suits with Sappho, Phoebus, suits with thee;
The gift, the giver, and the god agree."

But why, alas, relentless youth, ah, why
To distant seas must tender Sappho fly?
Thy charms than those may far more powerful be,
And Phoebus' self is less a god to me.
Ah, canst thou doom me to the rocks and sea,
O far more faithless and more hard than they?
Ah, canst thou rather see this tender breast
Dashed on these rocks than to thy bosom pressed?
This breast, which once, in vain! you liked so well;
Where the Loves played, and where the Muses dwell.
Alas, the Muses now no more inspire;
Untuned my lute, and silent is my lyre:

My languid numbers have forgot to flow,
And fancy sinks beneath the weight of woe.

Ye Lesbian virgins and ye Lesbian dames,
Themes of my verse and objects of my flames,
No more your groves with my glad songs shall ring;
No more these hands shall touch the trembling string:
My Phaon's fled, and I those arts resign:
(Wretch that I am, to call that Phaon mine!)
Return, fair youth, return, and bring along
Joy to my soul and vigour to my song.
Absent from thee, the poet's flame expires;
But ah, how fiercely burn the lover's fires!
Gods, can no prayers, no signs, no numbers move
One savage heart, or teach it how to love?
The winds my prayers, my sighs, my numbers bear;
The flying winds have lost them all in air.
Or when, alas, shall more auspicious gales
To these fond eyes restore thy welcome sails?
If you return, ah, why these long delays?
Poor Sappho dies while careless Phaon stays.
O launch the bark, nor fear the watery plain:
Venus for thee shall smoothe her native main.
O launch thy bark, secure of prosperous gales:
Cupid for thee shall spread the swelling sails.
If you will fly — (yet ah, what cause can be,
Too cruel youth, that you should fly from me?)
If not from Phaon I must hope for ease,
Ah, let me seek it from the raging seas;
To raging seas unpitied I'll remove;
And either cease to live or cease to love.

Ovid's Heroic Epistle, XV.
translated by Alexander Pope, 1707

METRICAL TABLES
AND
METRICAL INDEX

Prepared by
William E. McCulloh
Kenyon College

The reader's sense for the dynamism of a Greek poem is enhanced if he is able to feel the grouping of the words into their appropriate metrical (i.e., musical) phrases. The verse patterns available to the Greek lyric poet were of unique abundance and intricacy. The tables and index below have accordingly been provided for the sake of the reader who knows enough Greek to pronounce it and piece out the sense, but who has no experience with meters. Anyone who seeks a proper introduction to the subject should start with *The Meters of Greek and Latin Poetry*, by James W. Halporn, Martin Ostwald, and Thomas G. Rosenmeyer (Bobbs Merrill, 1963).*

Ancient Greek verse was structured by the relative lengths of the syllables in a line, not by the relative stresses. Syllables were of roughly two kinds: long, and short. A long syllable was approximately equal to two shorts. With a few exceptions, syllables containing the vowels η and ω, dipththongs, and "iota subscripts" were always long. α, ι, and υ were sometimes long, sometimes short, depending on the word. ε and ο in themselves were short. But when any short vowel was immediately followed by two consonants (either in the same word, or at the beginning of the next) the combination almost invariably — for Sappho — produced a long syllable.

Note these "irregularities": (1) A short syllable, if it was the last syllable in the line, was allowed to stand in place of a long syllable. (2) If one vowel was immediately followed (in the next syllable) by another vowel, the two could, on occasion, be slurred together — even from the end of one word to the beginning of the next. (3) At certain points in some verse forms (usually the beginning) either long or short syllables could be used. The sign for such a place in the line is x.

The poems may have been divided into seven books, of which the first four each had its own verse-form. The tables below follow this sevenfold division, with an eighth group for poems of uncertain location. The classifications by book (including the group of uncertain location) are made on the basis of the Lobel-Page edition, except for the following: 2, 13, 15,

* See also Denys Page's "Appendix on Metres" in *Sappho and Alcaeus*.

16, 20, 32, 34, 40, 41, 50, 55, 63, 64b, 65, 69, 70, 74, 75, 76, 88, 97, 99, 101, 102, 103, 106, 120, 122, 124, 125, 126, 136, 138, 144, 158.

I have tried to include the meters for as many of the fragments as seems worthwhile. For some very brief fragments the classification will hardly serve as more than an indication of the books to which they belonged. A number of lines are of doubtful metrical character. Thirteen fragments have been classified only by group (V, VII, or VIII) without indication of metrical pattern. Note: VI here = L-P's VII; VII here = L-P's IX.*

An index to the classification of all fragments follows the tables.

Signs: — long syllable
 ∪ short syllable
 x either long or short (*syllaba anceps*)
 | end of metrical phrase within the line
 ∪∪ either two shorts or one long

(Note: spacing has sometimes been employed to suggest grouping of smaller metrical units within the line.)

Book I: Poems in Sapphic stanza. The stanza is of four lines:

$$- \cup - x - \cup \cup - \cup - -$$
$$- \cup - x - \cup \cup - \cup - -$$
$$- \cup - x - \cup \cup - \cup - -$$
$$- \cup \cup - -$$

Frr. 5, 7, 9, 13, 14, 15, 17, 27, 28, 29, 30, 34, 38, 39?, 40, 41, 45, 50, 53, 84, 85, 86, 89, 102, 103, 104, 107, 110, 111, 115, 116, 125, 131, 134, 136?, 139, 141, 142, 143, 144?, 145

Book II: Poems in (so-called) Aeolic dactylic pentameter:
$$x x - \cup \cup \quad - \cup \cup \quad - \cup \cup \quad - \cup -$$
Frr. 8, 10, 54, 62, 68, 74, 83, 92 (text corrupt), 99, 126, 138?, 147

Book III: Poems in Greater Asclepiads:
$$x x - \cup \cup - \quad - \cup \cup - \quad - \cup \cup - \quad \cup -$$
Frr. 21, 26, 42, 73 (only last line), 75, 80, 87

Book IV: Poems in Ionic tetrameters of the following type:
$$x - \cup \cup - \quad - \cup \cup - \quad - \cup \cup - \quad \cup - -$$

* Page holds that there were nine books. His VI and VIII are not represented here.

Frr. 95, 96, 114, 117, 118, 119, 121, 140

Book V: Poems in variously composed stanzas.

    (1) Glyconics: x x – ∪ ∪   – ∪ –
Frr. 3, 36? (line 2: see I), 113 (only lines 1, 2, and 6)

      (2) Glyconics with units added at beginning and end:
         – ∪ – | x x – ∪ ∪   – ∪ – cretic | glyconic
         x x – ∪ ∪   – ∪ –   glyconic
         x x – ∪ ∪   – ∪ – | ∪ – – glyconic | bacchiac
Frr. 22, 69 (in second and third stanzas the "dactyl," or – ∪ ∪,
of the glyconic changes position with its neighbor on either
side), 133 (line 1 is last of stanza; "dactyl" is moved one position later in line 3)

      (3) x x – ∪ ∪   – ∪ –   glyconic
         x x – ∪ ∪   – ∪ –   glyconic
         x x – ∪ ∪   – ∪ ∪   – ∪ – glyconic with "in-
         serted dactyl"
Fr. 24

No meters given for the following members of Book V: 23 (text
very doubtfully restored by Edmonds), 90.

Book VI: The sole representative of this book seems to be Fr. 31:
     ∪ – ∪ – ∪ – – | ∪ ∪ – ∪ – ∪ – –

Book VII: Wedding songs in various meters:
    (1) Dactylic hexameters:
 – ∪ ∪   – ∪ ∪   – ∪ ∪   – ∪ ∪   – ∪ ∪   – –
Frr. 49, 94, 132 (text of line 2 is corrupt)

      (2) Miscellaneous lines of dactylic character:
         52 like VIII 4
         58 – –   – ∪ ∪   – –
           ∪ – ∪ –
           – – ∪ ∪   – ∪ ∪   – –
           ∪ – ∪ –
           (corrupt)
           – – ∪ ∪   – ∪ ∪   – –
         61 x x – ∪ ∪   – ∪ ∪   – –
         67 – ∪ ∪   – ∪ ∪   – ∪ ∪   – ∪ –

      (3) – ∪ ∪ –   ∪ – – | – ∪ ∪ –   ∪ – –
         – ∪ ∪ –   ∪ – – | – ∪ ∪ –   ∪ – –
         – ∪ ∪ –   ∪ – – | – ∪ ∪ –   ∪ – –
         – ∪ ∪ –   ∪ – –

$$− \cup \cup − \quad \cup − \cup −$$
$$− \cup − \cup \cup − \cup −$$
$$− \cup \cup − \quad \cup − −$$
$$− \cup \cup − \quad \cup − \cup − \quad \text{Fr. 57}$$

(4) $− \cup \cup − \quad − \cup \cup − \quad − \cup \cup − \quad \cup − −$

Fr. 66 (text corrupt, esp. line 2). Also 43 in VIII

No meters given for the following members of Book VII: 19, 56, 60.

Book VIII: Fragments of uncertain location. (The grouping provided here may suggest some interrelationships between adjacent verse-forms.)

    (1) Glyconics $\times \times − \cup \cup \quad − \cup −$ and Pherecratics $\times \times − \cup \cup \quad − −$.

Note: as indicated under V 2, the "dactyl" may occur earlier or later in the line on occasion.

Frr. 1 (gl.), 48 (gl.), 65 (lines 1 and 2 gl.; line 3 ph.), 79 (lines 1, 3, and 4 gl.; line 2 ph.), 88 (lines 2 and 3 gl.; in lines 1 and 4, an extra syllable at the end), 128 (lines 2, 3, and 4 gl.; line 1 ph.), 148 (gl.), 150 (gl.).

    (2) $\times \times − \cup \cup \quad − \cup \cup \quad − \cup −$ Fr. 25

    (3) $\cup \cup − \cup \cup \quad − \cup −$
$$\cup \cup − \cup − − \cup \cup \quad − \cup −$$
$$\cup \cup − \cup \cup \quad − \cup − ?$$
$$\cup \cup − \cup \cup − \quad \cup − −$$

Fr. 16. Chiefly glyconics?

    (4) $\times \times − \cup \cup \quad − \cup \cup \quad − \cup \cup \quad − −$

Frr. 18, 109? (52 in VII)

    (5) Dactylic hexameter:
$$− \underset{\smile\smile}{} \quad − \underset{\smile\smile}{} \quad − \underset{\smile\smile}{} \quad − \underset{\smile\smile}{} \quad − \cup \cup − −$$

Frr. 11, 77

    (6) Elegiac couplets:
$$− \underset{\smile\smile}{} \quad − \underset{\smile\smile}{} \quad − \underset{\smile\smile}{} \quad − \underset{\smile\smile}{} \quad − \cup \cup − −$$
$$− \underset{\smile\smile}{} \quad − \underset{\smile\smile}{} \quad − \mid − \cup \cup − \cup \cup −$$

Frr. 120, 124. (Cf. 2)

    (7) Miscellaneous lines of dactylic character:
      2 Cf. line 2 in VIII 6
      46 $− − \cup \cup \quad − \cup \cup \quad − − − \cup \underset{\smile}{}$

51 − ∪ ∪ − ∪ ∪ − ∪ −
93 ∪ ∪ − ∪ ∪ − ∪ − (gl.)
   − − − ∪ ∪ −
   ∪ ∪ − ∪ ∪ − ∪ ∪ − ∪ −
   − ∪ − ∪ ∪ − ∪ ∪ −
101 − ∪ ∪ − ∪ ∪ − ∪ ∪ − ∪ ∪ − −
108 − ∪ − ∪ ∪ − ∪ ∪ − −
129a − ∪ ∪ − −
146 − ∪ ∪ − −
151 − − ∪ ∪ − ∪ ∪ −
154 − ∪ ∪ − ∪ ∪ −
155 − ∪ ∪ − −
156 − − ∪ ∪ − ∪ ∪ −
157 − ∪ ∪ − −

(8) − ∪ ∪ − − | − ∪ ∪ − −
    ∪ ∪ − − − − − ∪ ∪ − ?

Fr. 98

(9) − − ∪ ∪ − −
    − − ∪ − −
    − − ∪ − − − − − ∪ ∪ − −
    − − ∪ ∪ − −
    − − ∪ − −
    − − ∪ − − − ∪ ∪ − ∪ − −
    − − −

Fr. 59

(10) − ∪ − ∪ − − ∪ ∪ − ∪ −   lines 1, 2, 4
     − ∪ ∪ − ∪ − − − ∪ − ∪   line 3
     − − − ∪ ∪ − − −   line 5

Fr. 70 (Cf. 97) In the Lobel-Page arrangement of the text, this poem belongs in II.

(11) Alcaic stanza:
     x − ∪ − x − ∪ ∪ − ∪ −
     x − ∪ − x − ∪ ∪ − ∪ −
     x − ∪ − x − ∪ − −
     − ∪ ∪ − ∪ ∪ − ∪ − −

Frr. 81 (incomplete), 82b. (The first two lines of 82 differ from the first two of an Alcaic stanza only by an extra syllable at the end of each.) Cf. 152.

(12) x − ∪ − − − ∪ ∪ − ∪ ∪ −

Frr. 20, 32

(13) − ∪ − − − ∪ ∪ − ∪ ∪ − ∪ − −

Fr. 71

$$(14)\ x - \cup - \cup \cup - \cup - \cup - -$$

Frr. 47, 72. Cf. 122, 130.

$$(15)\ - \cup - \cup - \cup - - - - \cup - \cup - -$$

Fr. 112. Cf. 153.

$$(16)\ - \cup - \quad \cup - - \quad - \cup - \quad \cup - -$$

Fr. 44.

$$(17)\ x - \cup \cup - \quad \cup - -$$

Fr. 6.

$$(18)\ - \quad - \cup \cup - \quad \cup - \cup - -$$
$$- \quad - \cup \cup - \quad \cup - \cup - -$$
$$- \quad - \cup \cup - \quad - \cup \cup - \quad \cup - -$$
$$- \quad - \cup \cup - \quad - \cup \cup - \quad \cup - -$$
$$- \quad - \cup \cup - \quad - \cup \cup - \quad \cup - -$$

Fr. 64.

(19) Lesser Asclepiads:

$$x\,x - \cup \cup - \quad - \cup \cup - \quad \cup -$$

Frr. 4? 12? (incomplete), 33? 106, 127 (line 1), 137, 149? (incomplete). Cf. 158.

$$(20)\ x\,x - \cup \cup - \quad - \cup \cup - \quad - \cup \cup - -$$

Fr. 35.

$$(21)\ \cup \cup - - \quad \cup \cup - - \quad \cup \cup - -$$

Fr. 78.

Other fragments of uncertain location: 37, 43 (like VII 4), 55, 63, 76 (latter part of III?), 91, 100, 105, 123, 135.

INDEX

CONCORDANCES

ABBREVIATIONS

Alc. — Alcaeus

Sa. — Sappho

Suppl. — Supplement to Diehl's ANTHOLOGIA LYRICA
GRAECA

om. — omitted

Inc. — *Incertum Utrius Auctoris Fragmenta,* a section of
fragments attributed to Sappho and Alcaeus but whose
authorship is in question. Lobel and Page, pp. 292–297.

(App.) — the appendix of Lobel's edition

Fr. Mel. Mon. Adesp. — *Fragmenta Melica Monodica Ades-
pota,* a collection of melic fragments whose authorship
is in question; found at the end of Diehl's Melic Poets.

A CONCORDANCE TO BARNSTONE

BARNSTONE	DIEHL	EDMONDS	LOBEL AND PAGE
1	103	80	118
2	om.	1a	om.
3	*Suppl.* pp. 39, 70	om.	98a
4	108	74	120
5	27	38	16
6	94	111	om.
7	19	27	38
8	50	54	47
9	2	2	31
10	47	53	52
11	118	139	143
12	113	78	145
13	11	12	160
14	4	3	34
15	15	19	123
16	Alc. 94	94	Alc. 347b
17	13	16	42
18	121	138	136
19	133	32	104b
20	156	133	om.
21	56	69	54
22	98	86	96
23	95	82	92
24	96	83	94
25	137	81	130, 131
26	40, 41	48	49
27	34a	43	24a
28	1	1	1
29	*Suppl.* p. 30	4, 6	2
30	28	40	17
31	114	135	102
32	156	134	om.
33	110	75	159
34	om.	31	198
35	107	103	140
36	99	87	101
37	87	123	134
38	8	7, 8	40
39	9	9	33

BARNSTONE	DIEHL	EDMONDS	LOBEL AND PAGE
40	145	24	*Inc.* 23
41	om.	33	200
42	57	68	53
43	90	101	128
44	154	129	127
45	10	10	32
46	134	128	126
47	144b	126	133 (16A)
48	143	55	144
49	116, 117	150, 151	105a, 105c
50	om.	30	185
51	101	67	125
52	127	161	115
53	39	47	30
54	54	65	43
55	om.	147	om.
56	130	163	113
57	128	155, 156, 158	112
58	123	148 (ll. 1-7)	111
59	135, 136	146	141
60	128, 129	160, 162	116, 117
61	124	154	110
62	46	52	51
63	om.	84A	197
64	88, 93	112, 114	154, *Inc.* 16
65	om.	157	om.
66	131	164	114
67	53	159	107
68	55a, 55b	66	44
69	98 (ll. 21-9)	86A (App.)	96 (ll. 21-9)
70	48	89	48
71	150	121	155
72	144a	125	133 (16)
73	61	98	57
74	45	51	*Inc.* 5
75	62	73	*Inc.* 11
76	Alc. 9a	70	Alc. 349b
77	119	140	142
78	86	122	135
79	92	100	148
80	58	71	55
81	151	120	138
82	Alc. 63, Sa. 149	Alc. 124, Sa. 119	Alc. 384, Sa. 137
83	49	58	50
84	36	45	22
85	20	23	36
86	31	41	20
87	60	72	56
88	om.	110	204
89	17	20	39
90	85	105	100

BARNSTONE	DIEHL	EDMONDS	LOBEL AND PAGE
91	142	21	152
92	42	56, 57	46
93	138, 139	61, 60, 59, 62	156, 167
94	115	148 (ll. 9-11)	106
95	80	117	81b
96	63	115	82a
97	141	93	*Inc.* 5 (l. 2)
98	126	137	158
99	156B	50A (App.)	139
100	om.	90	196
101	51	142	*Inc.* 25
102	18	22	129 (l. 2)
103	147	29	163
104	14	18	37
105	111	107	122
106	140	96	*Inc.* 5 (l. 3)
107	37	13	26 (ll. 2-4)
108	52	106	146
109	125, 106	141, 141A	149, 151
110	38	46	27
111	35	44	23
112	152	130	132
113	*Suppl.* pp. 39, 70	om.	98b
114	70	om.	71
115	25	36	5
116	26	37	15
117	65a	118	58
118	67	118B (App.)	63
119	66	118A (App.)	62
120	159	145	om.
121	64	116	91
122	om.	113A, 113B	*Inc.* 18
123	om.	91	201
124	158	144	om.
125	om.	om.	*Inc.* 27
126	102	152	Alc. 304
127	105	97	166
128	100	99	121
129	om.	28	172, 188
130	146	124	129 (l. 1)
131	12	14	41
132	120	149	104a
133	97	85	95
134	32	42	21
135	109	108	150
136	om.	11	193
137	59	76, 77	147
138	*Fr. Mel. Mon. Adesp.* 18	*Lyra Graeca* III, p. 438	om.
139	24	34	4
140	68	om.	65

BARNSTONE	DIEHL	EDMONDS	LOBEL AND PAGE
141	7	5	35
142	37	15	26 (ll. 11-12)
143	14	17	37
144	3	26	165
145	27b	39	16 (l. 32)
146	43	49	om.
147	44	50	45
148	om.	64	191
149	112	79	164
150	104	95	178
151	155	127	124
152	156A	132	162
153	153	131	119
154	122	153	109
155	16	177	157
156	133a	191	192
157	21	25	168
158	132b	136	*Inc.* 24

CONCORDANCE TO DIEHL

Diehl	Barnstone	Diehl	Barnstone
1	28	48	70
2	9	49	83
3	144	50	8
4	14	51	101
7	141	52	108
8	38	53	67
9	39	54	54
10	45	55a	68
11	13	55b	68
12	131	56	21
13	17	57	42
14	104, 143	58	80
15	15	59	137
16	155	60	87
17	89	61	73
18	102	62	75
19	7	63	96
20	85	64	121
21	157	65a	117
25	115	66	119
26	116	67	118
27	5	70	114
27b	147	80	95
28	30	85	90
31	86	86	78
32	134	87	37
34a	27	88	64
35	111	90	43
36	84	92	79
37	107, 142	93	64
38	110	94	6
39	53	95	23
40	26	96	24
41	26	97	133
42	92	98	22, 69
43	146	99	36
44	147	100	128
45	74	101	51
46	62	102	126
47	10	103	1

DIEHL	BARNSTONE	DIEHL	BARNSTONE
104	150	136	59
105	127	137	25
106	109	138	93
107	35	139	93
108	4	140	106
109	135	141	97
110	33	142	91
111	105	143	48
112	149	144a	72
113	12	144b	47
114	31	145	40
115	94	146	130
116	49	147	103
117	49	149	82
118	11	150	71
119	77	151	81
120	132	152	112
121	18	153	153
122	154	154	44
123	58	155	151
124	61	156	20, 32
125	109	156A	152
126	98	156B	99
127	52	158	124
128	57, 60	159	120
129	60	Supplement:	
130	56	p. 30	29
131	66	pp. 39, 70	3, 113
132b	158	Alc. 9A	76
133	19	Alc. 63	82
133A	156	Alc. 94	16
134	46	*Fr. Mel. Mon.*	138
135	59	*Adesp.* 18	

CONCORDANCE TO EDMONDS

Edmonds	Barnstone	Edmonds	Barnstone
1	28	42	134
1a	2	43	27
2	9	44	111
3	14	45	84
4	29	46	110
6	29	47	53
7	38	48	26
8	38	49	146
9	39	50	147
10	45	51	74
11	136	52	62
12	13	53	10
13	107	54	8
14	131	55	48
15	142	56	92
16	17	57	92
17	143	58	83
18	104	59	93
19	15	60	93
20	89	61	93
21	91	62	93
22	102	64	148
23	85	65	54
24	40	66	68
25	157	67	51
26	144	68	42
27	7	69	21
28	129	70	76
29	103	71	80
30	50	72	87
31	34	73	75
32	19	74	4
33	41	75	33
34	139	76	137
36	115	77	137
37	116	78	12
38	5	79	149
39	145	80	1
40	30	81	25
41	86	82	23

EDMONDS	BARNSTONE	EDMONDS	BARNSTONE
83	24	131	153
84A	63	132	152
85	133	133	20
86	22	134	32
87	36	135	31
89	70	136	158
90	100	137	98
91	123	138	18
93	97	139	11
94	16	140	77
95	150	141	109
96	106	141A	109
97	127	142	101
98	73	144	124
99	128	145	120
100	79	146	59
101	43	147	55
103	35	148	58, 94
105	90	149	132
106	108	150	49
107	105	151	49
108	135	152	126
110	88	153	154
111	6	154	61
112	64	155	57
113A	122	156	57
113B	122	157	65
114	64	158	57
115	96	159	67
116	121	160	60
117	95	161	52
118	117	162	60
119	82	163	56
120	81	164	66
121	71	177	155
122	78	191	156
123	37	Appendix:	
124	130	50A	99
125	72	86A	69
126	47	118A	119
127	151	118B	118
128	46	Alc. 124	82
129	44	*Lyra Graeca* III,	138
130	112	p. 438	

CONCORDANCE TO LOBEL AND PAGE

Lobel and Page	Barnstone	Lobel and Page	Barnstone
1	28	57	73
2	29	58	117
4	139	62	119
5	115	63	118
15	116	65	140
16	5, 145	71	114
17	30	81b	95
20	86	82a	96
21	134	91	121
22	84	92	23
23	111	94	24
24a	27	95	133
26	107, 142	96	22, 69
27	110	98a	3
30	53	98b	113
31	9	100	90
32	45	101	36
33	39	102	31
34	14	104a	132
36	85	104b	19
37	104, 143	105a	49
38	7	105c	49
39	89	106	94
40	38	107	67
41	131	109	154
42	17	110	61
43	54	111	58
44	68	112	57
45	147	113	56
46	92	114	66
47	8	115	52
48	70	116	60
49	26	117	60
50	83	118	1
51	62	119	153
52	10	120	4
53	42	121	128
54	21	122	105
55	80	123	15
56	87	124	151

LOBEL AND PAGE	BARNSTONE	LOBEL AND PAGE	BARNSTONE
126	46	125	51
127	44	162	152
128	43	163	103
129	102, 130	164	149
130	25	165	144
131	25	166	127
132	112	167	93
133	47, 72	168	157
134	37	172	129
135	78	178	150
136	18	185	50
137	82	188	129
138	81	191	148
139	99	192	156
140	35	193	136
141	59	196	100
142	77	197	63
143	11	198	34
144	48	200	41
145	12	201	123
146	108	204	88
147	137	Alc. 304	126
148	79	Alc. 347b	16
149	109	Alc. 349b	76
150	135	Alc. 384	82
151	109	*Incertum:*	
152	91	5	74, 97, 106
154	64	11	75
155	71	16	64
156	93	18	122
157	155	23	40
158	98	24	158
159	33	25	101
160	13	27	125

CONCORDANCE TO MISCELLANEOUS TEXTS

OTHER	BARNSTONE	EDMONDS	DIEHL	LOBEL AND PAGE
Bowra, p. 196	29	4, 6	*Suppl.* p. 30	2
Bowra, p. 221	53	47	39	30
Lobel, p. 80	69	86A (App.)	98 (ll. 21-9)	96 (ll. 21-9)
Page 1	28	1	1	1
Page 2	9	2	2	31
Page 5	115	36	25	5
Page 17	30	40	28	17
Robinson 122	100	90	om.	196
Treu, p. 7	126	152	102	Alc. 304
Treu, p. 16	125	om.	om.	*Inc.* 27